#startupeverywhere

Startup Guide Zürich

Editor: Jenna van Uden
Copyeditor: Marissa van Uden
Proofreader: Ted Hermann
Writers: Josh Raisher, Mark Fletcher, Charmaine Li and John Sperryn
Photographer: Jasmin Frei/Pep Shot
Researcher: Eglė Duleckytė
Production Manager: Tim Rhodes
Design: Ines Pedro

Illustrations by Joana Carvalho

Zürich Team: Carmen Romero, Zsófia Molnár, David Emmerth, Lorena Kreis, Tauras Sinkevicius, Christoph Birkholz, Ruth Armale, Thomas Patzko, Anais Sägesser, Olmar Albers, Stefan Honegger and Katka Letzing

Research by Impact Hub Zürich, Business and Economic Development at the Office for Economy and Labour of the Canton of Zürich, Economic Development of the City of Zürich and Greater Zürich Area

Additional photography by
Daniela Carducci and Unsplash.com
Printed in Berlin, Germany by
Medialis-Offsetdruck GmbH
Heidelbergerstraße 65, 12435 Berlin

Published by Startup Guide World IVS
Kanonbådsvej 2, 1437 Copenhagen K
info@startupguide.world

Visit: startupguide.world

ISBN 978-3-947624-00-3

STARTUP GUIDE ZÜRICH

STARTUP GUIDE ZÜRICH

In partnership with **Impact Hub Zürich**

Proudly Supported by

 Canton of Zurich
Department for Economic Affairs
Office for Economy and Labour

Sissel Hansen
/ Startup Guide

As the homeland of Dadaism, which was founded a little more than one hundred years ago, Zürich has definitely been an attractive spot for international people. It feels like the city still has the independent and liberated spirit that allowed it to gather multidisciplinary artists who expressed their worldviews during the late 1910s. And in the twenty-first century, it has become known for fostering innovation and being open to cultural differences.

For the last few years, Zürich has been high on the quality-of-life index. According to thelocal.ch, it's one of the best cities for expats to live in, and timeout.com rates it as one of the priciest but most livable places on the planet.

When thinking about Zürich, and about Switzerland as a whole, what comes to mind is an efficient, eco-friendly and balanced place. Most of the startups featured in this guide (such as ElectricFeel, ImagineCargo and Urban Farmers) are concerned with sustainability and with maintaining eco-friendly and bio-friendly processes – a few of the main focuses of the Zürich entrepreneurship ecosystem.

The Swiss city leads in innovation in different verticals. For example, the Zürchers have recently voted for and accepted a parliamentary postulate to examine a Basic Income pilot project in two districts of the city. The future of work and living is being experimented with, which is a clear indicator of a strong economy, strong education, and residents with a strong sense of responsibility.

A very important part of Zürich's entrepreneurial success is the university: ETH Zürich is the main generator of startups in Zürich. Since 1996, there have been 380 spin-offs established at ETH Zürich, with 25 of them established in 2017 alone. This is the unmistakable sign of a prosperous entrepreneurial ecosystem in a city, and, by the looks of it, ETH Zürich is only just getting started. The ETH Entrepreneur Club and its new coworking space will most definitely create more room for future entrepreneurs to grow.

I feel that Zürich, the capital of banking and finance in Europe, has an incredible power in shaping and balancing the future of work and life in a very bright way. It is a great example of how, by investing in quality, time, sustainability and talent, we could all achieve the happy medium between working and living – and do so in the best way possible. David Allemann, the cofounder of On (featured in this guide), says, "You can't be too fast when it comes to innovation." This is a great example of how Swiss people perceive their lives.

Sissel
Founder and CEO

Carmen Walker Späh and Corine Mauch

The region of Zürich is more than just the center of the Swiss startup scene. Thanks to our unique innovation ecosystem, it's also drawing increasing attention internationally as an attractive location for young enterprises. Everything in Zürich is within easy reach – the airport, our renowned universities, our numerous research centers and international companies – and all set in a hip environment that comes with a vibrant creative-industries sector and a high quality of life. In short, the City and the Canton of Zürich are excellent places for exploring and promoting innovative ideas in collaboration with a wealth of creative people.

Switzerland is not only the land of mountains, lakes and watches; it's also the land of company founders. In the Canton of Zürich alone, close to seven thousand companies are founded every year. Our lively startup scene is also very positive in macroeconomic terms because today's startups constitute the foundation of our future economy. The City and the Canton of Zürich are highly committed to providing the best possible conditions for startup companies. But, since nobody is perfect, we are also very interested in continuously improving Zürich's locational appeal, and we are always open to feedback and suggestions.

In today's digital world, accessing data via our smartphones is easy. However, faced with the flood of data on the web, acquiring a detailed overview on a particular topic and retrieving focused information can present a challenge. This is where the Startup Guide comes in: devised as a practical navigation aid for Zürich's startup ecosystem, the guide breaks new ground for networking and sharing information within the startup scene. We congratulate the creators of the Startup Guide on their thoroughly researched and successful handbook.

Government Councillor Carmen Walker Späh   City Mayor Corine Mauch
Department for Economic Affairs, Canton of Zürich   City of Zürich

Local Ecosystem

[Facts & Figures]
- Zürich is a leading center of finance, knowledge and industry with outstanding universities and research institutions, a lively startup culture and an excellent quality of life. According to the *Financial Times*, Zürich ranks sixth in the "fDi European Cities and Regions of the Future 2016/2017."
- The city of Zürich regularly occupies the top rankings of world cities based on quality of life, and, according to the 2018 Global Talent Competitiveness Index, it attracts more global talents than any other city.
- Zürich's well-developed infrastructure – such as direct connections to the airport and public transport – make the region one of the most attractive business locations in the world.
- Zürich is one of Europe's most important financial centers. The finance sector generates around a third of the wealth and a fifth of the jobs in the city.
- The Swiss Federal Institute of Technology ETH generates twenty-five startups each year, of which 90 percent remain in successful operation over the next five years.
- In the city of Zürich, 385,000 foreign workers are employed, with 90 percent employed in the service sector.

[Notable Startup Activity·]
- In the Canton of Zürich, more than 7,000 enterprises are founded every year.
- Wingtra, a spin-off from the engineering school ETH Zürich, raised €5.8 million, bringing total funds raised to €10 million (CHF 11.5 million).
- Guuru, a live-chat startup, has raised €688,000 (CHF 800,000) in funding to facilitate expansion into the DACH region.
- RosieReality raised €565,000 ($700,000) in seed funding to teach robotics to children.
- In 2016, Heptares acquired G7 Therapeutics, a spin-off from the University of Zürich for CHF 12 million.
- In 2017, Neurimmune, a spin-off from the University of Zürich, raised $150 million to fund its growth strategy.
- Forty-three of the Top 100 Startups 2017 originated from the Canton of Zürich.

Sources: stadt-zuerich.ch, zh.ch, startupticker.ch, greaterZüricharea.ch, startup.ch/top100 and tatacommunications.com/press-release/2018-global-talent-competitiveness-index

[City:] # Zürich, Switzerland

[Statistics:]
GDP: **€121.38 billion**
Unemployment rate: **3.5 percent**
Land area: **1,728.9 km²**
Population: **1,482,650**
Percentage of foreign population: **26 percent**
Four national languages: **German, French, Italian, Romansh**

Local Community Partner / Impact Hub Zürich

What does it take for a startup scene to grow? We believe shared knowledge, a network for collaboration, and a supportive ecosystem are all key ingredients. We offer these elements in our entrepreneurial community at Impact Hub Zürich. Our focus is on sustainable development and innovation – as defined by the UN sustainable development goals – and we believe that a deeply collaborative approach is needed to address the grand challenges of our time.

Impact Hub Zürich is part of a global network of around ninety Impact Hubs worldwide. However, it's not just the power of our global network that makes us strong; in order to evolve, our Hubs must also be locally rooted.

Switzerland offers a fertile ground for growth and is a leader in innovation. The number of companies founded in Switzerland has been rising steadily over recent years, with Zürich at the forefront of this growth. As an important financial home to many leading international corporations (including influential academic institutions such as ETH Zürich), the city plays a key role for the startup scene in Switzerland and, increasingly, worldwide. While Zürich's footprint on the startup map is still modest, it has been growing continuously over recent years.

We are happy and proud to be part of the Startup Guide Zürich, an important guide and inspiration for entrepreneurship in Switzerland. So let's zoom in to Zürich, that beautiful spot on the map by the river Limmat, and look at its most important players in the startup scene.

Christoph Birkholz

STARTUP
GUIDE
ZÜRICH

startups

programs

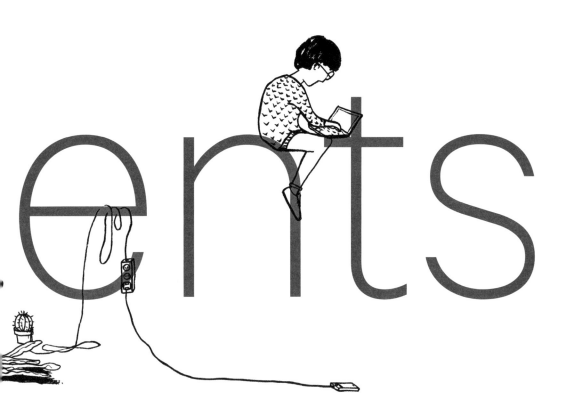

Intro to the City and the Region

Known globally as a leading financial center, Zürich is much more than a banking hub. It's a vibrant, creative hotspot that features extraordinary cultural diversity, a lively nightlife scene, political and economic stability, a high quality of life, and a flair for supporting innovative technologies and entrepreneurs from all over the world. Thanks to its location in the heart of Europe, Zürich is easy to reach from any of Switzerland's neighboring countries.

Set against the scenic backdrop of Lake Zürich and the Swiss Alps, Zürich boasts blissfully fresh, clean air and is home to more than 1,200 drinking fountains. Its charming Old Town is where history comes alive. Over the years, Zürich has evolved into a leading location for startups from a broad spectrum of industries, including ICT, fintech and biotech, just to mention a few. Though relatively small in size, the opportunities on offer in Zürich are abundant. As the economic motor that drives Switzerland, Zurich is a place of constant innovation, transformation and growth. With a tradition of offering resourceful minds the chance and the space to implement their ideas, it is not surprising that Zürich is now, more than ever, a city and region where doers, movers and shakers thrive.

Before You Come

First of all, make sure you have all the documents you need for your permit, depending on whether you already have a job contract or not and which country you're coming from. Permanent accommodation can take several months to organize, so it's a good idea to find temporary housing to start with. Zürich has a reputation for being one of the most expensive cities in the world, so have enough savings to survive the first few months. Although you can get by with English, it's a good idea to start acquiring some knowledge of German before arriving. Be aware that Switzerland has its own type of power plugs, so get converters before arrival. You can find more information about living in Zürich at welcome.zh.ch, zuerich.ch and zuerich.com. Finally, don't forget your hiking boots: Swiss mountains are a hiker's paradise, and Uetliberg, the city's local mountain, is right on Zürich's doorstep.

Cost of Living

Although life in Zürich can be expensive, its quality of life ranks as one of the best in the world. A room in a shared apartment can cost between CHF 400 and CHF 900 per month, depending on the area and the size of the room. One-bedroom apartments are usually between CHF 1,200 and CHF 1,500, while two-bedroom apartments average somewhere between CHF 1,500 and CHF 1,800. Eating out is quite expensive: expect to pay at least CHF 25 for dinner in an inexpensive restaurant without wine or other drinks. Depending on what you buy, CHF 500 per month should cover your grocery shopping. Health insurance is mandatory in Switzerland, and depending on the model and provider you choose, it can cost between CHF 250 and CHF 2,500 per month. Biking around in the city is by far the cheapest, quickest and healthiest option, and there are decent secondhand bikes available from around CHF 200. If you prefer public transportation, then you should definitely get a half-fare travel card for CHF 165 per year, which gives you a 50 percent discount on almost any public transport in the whole of Switzerland. A single tram ride in Zürich would then cost either CHF 2.30 or 3.10, and a return train to Basel would start at about CHF 34.

Cultural Differences

Swiss people are as diverse as any other nationality, but there are some typical characteristics that are helpful to know. First, Swiss people are very polite and cherish their privacy. For instance, you might see one of the country's seven Federal Councillors waiting for a train at Zürich Central Station. Most Swiss people will recognize them but never approach them, out of respect for their privacy. Rules and rule compliance are important to the Swiss: before crossing a street, almost every pedestrian will stop when the traffic light turns red, even if there are no cars in sight. One of the most important rules for getting along with the Swiss is to be punctual for meetings and private dates, and to let the person you're meeting know if you are running late, even if it's only five minutes.

Renting an Apartment

Renting an apartment in Zürich can be both easy and hard, depending on your needs and budget. If you're looking for a great location at a great price, get ready to compete with fifty other applicants, but if you're fine with living in a less central location, your chances of getting your desired apartment are much higher. Also, things are easier if you're just looking for a room in a shared apartment. The whole application process is, as most things are in Switzerland, very well organized. You see an ad, you visit the apartment at the designated visiting time, and, if you like the place, you fill out the form and submit it with your *Betreibungsauszug* (debt collection records) and criminal records certificate. After a few weeks you'll receive notification as to whether or not you got the apartment. The best places for finding an apartment are homegate. ch and immoscout24.ch, and for shared apartments visit wgzimmer.ch, flatfox.ch or ronorp.net/zuerich/immobilien.

See **Flats and Rentals** page **186**

Finding a Coworking Space

Zürich's coworking scene started ten years ago, with Citizen Space being the pioneer. Impact Hub Zürich, which focuses on community and collaboration, is arguably the largest coworking provider with four locations, one of which is Kraftwerk, a joint venture project between Impact Hub, digitalswitzerland, Engagement Migros and ewz. At Colab, Impact Hub's main location, coworkers and guests can enjoy one of the best coffees in town at its in-house cafe Auer & Co. Several other coworking spaces have popped up in Zürich, including Spaces, Hush, Rocket Hub, OfficeLab, Büro Züri, and Kampagnenforum. Coworking Switzerland provides a list of most of Zürich's coworking spaces at coworking.ch. Due to its small geographic size and excellent public transport system, the city's coworking scene is easily accessible, and visitors and locals alike can drop in at multiple locations to work, meet and connect.

See **Spaces** page **74**

Insurance

Basic health insurance is compulsory in Switzerland. The healthcare system is not free, and every insured person pays a monthly premium. The amount is made up of a basic insurance (mandatory) and supplementary coverage (voluntary, according to the individual's needs or wishes). Good resources to check are comparis.ch and priminfo.ch. As for social security, contributions are mandatory for every employee and employer. The employee's share gets deducted directly from the gross salary. If you're self-employed, the mandatory forms of insurance are the old age and survivors' insurance (AHV), disability insurance (IV) and income compensation (EO). To arrange these, you'll need to get in touch with Zürich's social insurance office, SVA (svazurich.ch). Additionally, you may want to consider taking out other insurances, such as a personal liability insurance and a household insurance. Contact one of the main Swiss insurance companies (e.g., AXA, Zürich, Allianz) for a consultation. Some of these insurance companies also offer startup packages.

See **Insurance Companies** page **187**

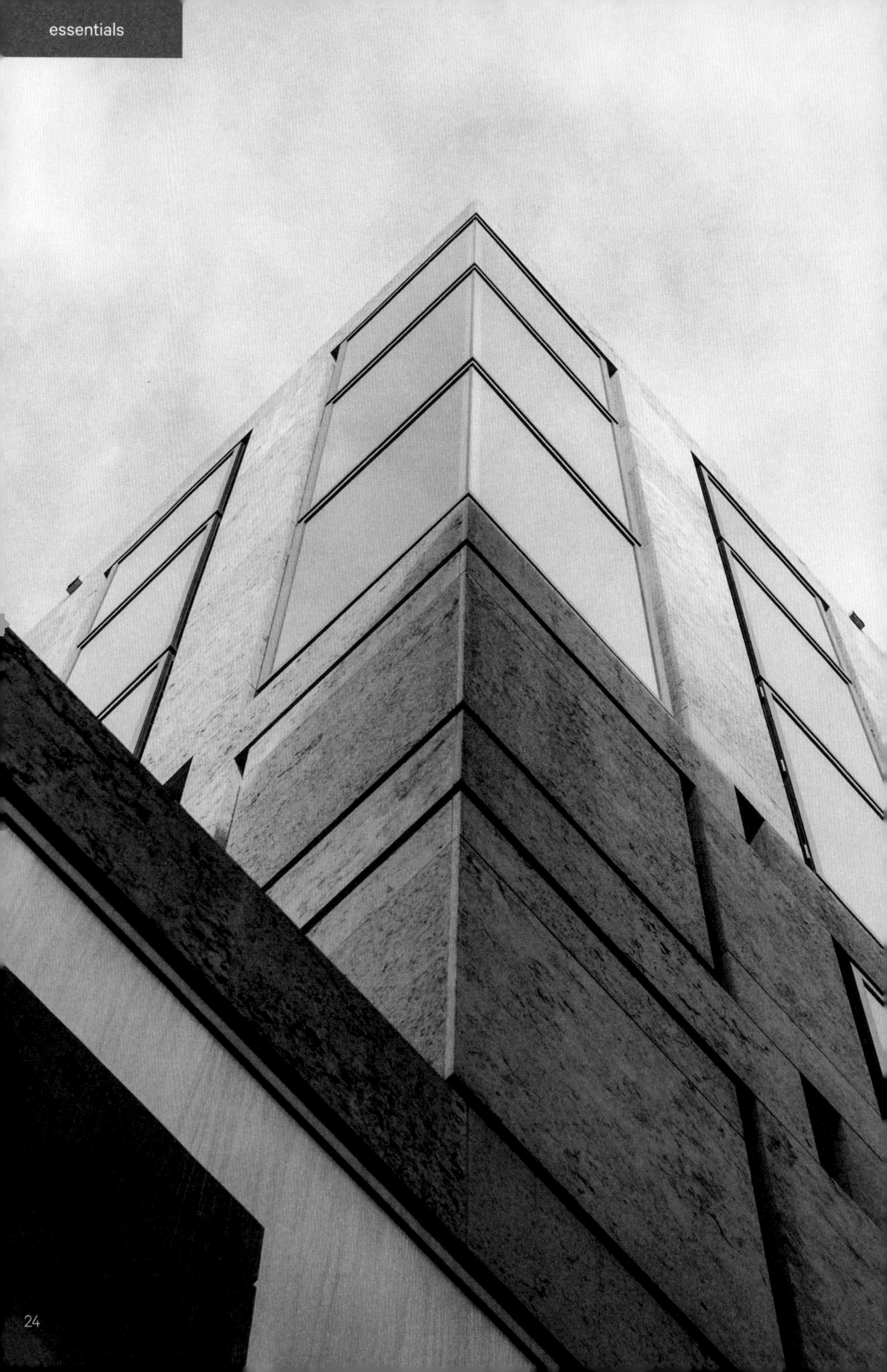

Visas and Work Permits

If you're an EU/EEA national, you're free to travel to Switzerland to live and work there. You're allowed to stay for up to three months without a permit, and you can apply for a temporary residence permit valid for an additional three months within any calendar year, provided you have the financial means to pay for your living expenses. You don't need a permit for short-term employment for up to three months; however, the employment needs to be registered. For employment lasting longer than three months, EU/EEA nationals require a residence permit. If you're not self-employed, you need a statement of engagement from the employer or a certificate of employment. If you're self-employed, you'll have to provide accounting records in order to prove that you can earn a decent living. Third-state nationals who want to work in Switzerland will need a residence permit. Whether or not you'll be granted authorization to work depends on existing work quotas, your education level and your work experience. Applications for self-employment for third-state nationals are evaluated based on the general economic interest. The website workpermits.zh.ch provides detailed information about work permits.

See **Important Government Offices** page **186**

Taxes

On an international scale, taxes in Switzerland are fairly moderate, both for individuals and companies. Due to Switzerland's federal structure (taxes are levied by the confederation, the 26 Cantons and the 2,255 municipalities), there are considerable differences depending on where you live. The tax rate in the Canton of Zürich is lower than the national average. In Switzerland, taxes are paid on income and wealth as well as on goods and services. In addition, most Cantons levy inheritance and gift taxes. Aside from where you live, the amount of tax you pay depends mainly on your income. Your assets, marital status and number of dependent children have a smaller impact. Residents or temporary residents in Switzerland are subject to unlimited tax liability (taxes apply to worldwide income and assets), as are companies with a registered office or administration in Switzerland. Limited tax liability applies to non-residents and foreign companies who hold real estate or a permanent establishment in Switzerland. Withholding taxes are not paid by the taxpayers themselves but directly by the employer, promoter or insurer, etc., prior to the deduction of the sum due.

Starting a Company

Starting a company is easy and straightforward in Switzerland. The legal form you choose for your company will determine whether you must register the business in the commercial register. A detailed checklist for founding a company is available at gruenden.ch and a good overview of the legal forms is available at startups.ch. Registration and the preliminary examination of the details are carried out by the commercial registry of the Canton where your company will be based. Visit *hra.zh.ch* or *gruenden.ch* for an overview of the processes in Zürich. If you're becoming a sole enterprise, a general partnership or a limited partnership, you'll need to apply for self-employment status at the *Ausgleichskasse*. You'll answer a questionnaire that will determine whether or not you will be granted the status. A person may be granted the status of self-employment if they are independent and work in their own name, for their own account and at their own economic risk.

See **Programs** page **56**

Opening a Bank Account

Zürich is still mostly a "cash" city. Credit cards will rarely be accepted for amounts smaller than CHF 20, while amounts larger than CHF 200 are mostly paid by card or bank transfer. To open a bank account, you'll need to bring proof of identity, proof of a valid Swiss residence, and your work permit or employment contract. Accounts typically take between one week and one month to become active, and once they're active, any requested credit cards or debit cards will arrive after seven or ten days. With a Swiss bank account, you'll have no ATM fees, but you may be charged an annual fee for administration depending on the average balance of your account. PostFinance is one of the cheapest when it comes to fees. There are some banks, such as Zürcher Kantonalbank, that offer special deals for startups.

See **Banks** page **185**

Getting Around

Your best options for getting around in Zürich are trams, buses, bicycles or walking. You will find the bus and tram schedules at online.fahrplan.zvv.ch. Tickets can be bought via the ZVV app (credit card required) or at the ticket vending machines you'll find at every bus stop, tram stop and train station. If you're planning to stay for a longer period of time, check out the official website of the Swiss Federal Railways (sbb.ch) for the "half-fare travel card" or, if you're under twenty-five years of age, get the discounted "Track 7" ticket. There are also regional or point-to-point travel cards if you take the same route regularly. A regular day pass for the city of Zürich costs CHF 8.80, or CHF 6.20 with a half-fare travel card. For trips to other cities, it's best to take a train. Swiss trams, buses and trains are usually very punctual and run regularly, and schedules are published on sbb.ch (or the SBB app). A piece of advice: do buy a ticket. Although you're not required to show your ticket when entering a bus or tram, if you're caught without a valid ticket, you'll be fined about CHF 100.

Telephone Contracts

The main telecommunication companies offering mobile phone services in Switzerland are Swisscom, Salt and Sunrise. Mobile prepaid cards and mobile subscriptions can be purchased online and in phone company stores. As a rule, the contract periods are twelve or twenty-four months. When choosing a provider, consider where you'll use your phone the most as pricing varies for roaming and high data usage. For a list of providers offering fiber-optic home internet within Zürich, visit meinzuerinet.ch.

Learning the Language

Grüezi! Swiss German refers to all Alemannic dialects spoken in the German-speaking part of Switzerland. On arrival, you may well discover that, regardless of how good your German is or how many hours you've spent in a language school, you still have problems understanding Swiss native speakers. Dialects from different regions (often heard on the radio and TV) can vary. The written language is Standard German, which is why language schools mainly teach Standard German. There are many language schools to choose from: Klubschule Migros and EB Zürich are popular adult education schools, Flying Teachers is affordable, and Unumondo offers unique learning methods. Other ways to pick up German are to read local newspapers such as NZZ or Tages-Anzeiger, join the Pestalozzi Bibliothek or Zentralbibliothek Zürich (Zürich Central Library), or watch Swiss television (srf.ch). Once you've mastered (Swiss) German, you might start learning French, Italian or Romansh, the other three official languages of Switzerland.

See **Language Schools** page **188**

Meeting People

During the warm summer months, the locals love to take a refreshing dip in the crystal-clear water of Lake Zürich, the river Limmat, one of the smaller lakes in the vicinity, or one of the many public outdoor swimming pools. Hiking is also very popular, and the city is home to a large number of public parks. In the evenings, people like to enjoy a drink in an outdoor bar, watch a movie in an open-air cinema, or attend open-air concerts and street festivals. During the colder months, when the mountains are covered in snow, residents leave the city to hit the slopes in one of the many ski resorts near Zürich. The city has events year round. A great place to find out about them is at zuerich.com, meetup.com or the online platform RON ORP (ronorp. net/zuerich), which also publishes a daily newsletter.

See **Startup Events** page **188**

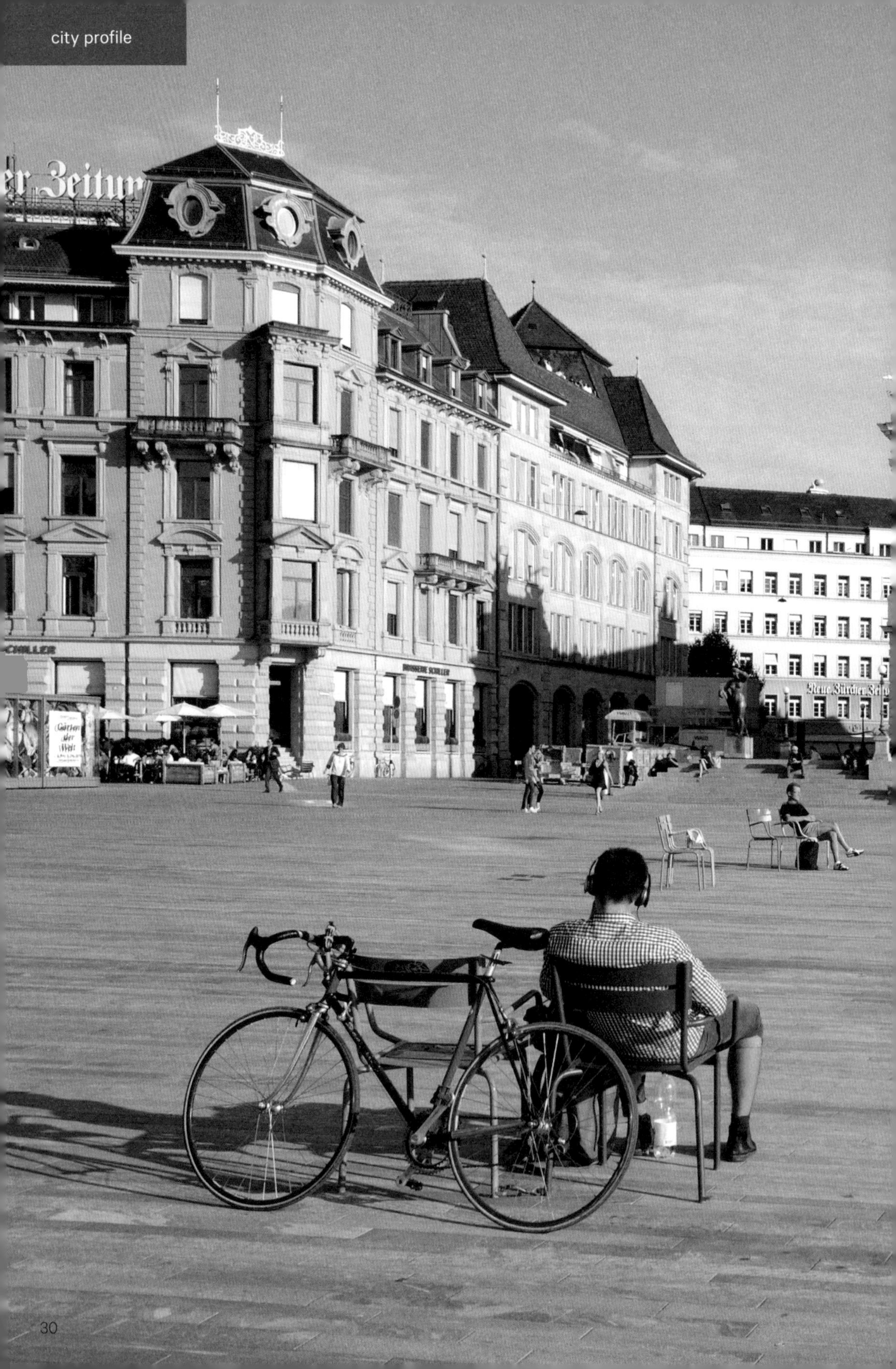

Zürich Facts and Figures

Zürich is one of the top twenty startup hubs in Europe (according to the Startup Heatmap Europe 2017), home to an increasing number of international startup headquarters. Young companies can count on the city's rich network of support in almost all areas, from financing and coworking to collaboration in R&D.

Leading in innovation and technology, it also has a strong cluster and industry diversity. The Zürich region boasts the highest density of creative industries and ICT clusters in Switzerland, and the cluster ecosystem is based on constructive coexistence and collaboration of domestic and international companies in Zürich.

Finance Cluster
Zürich is one of the most attractive financial centers in the world, ranking in Europe only behind London. As a consequence, numerous fintech, insurtech and regtech startups are entering the market and challenging the established leaders.

A few Key Players: Banks and Insurance companies, Swiss Finance Startups, Swiss Fintech Innovations, Swiss Finance + Technology Association.

Creative Industries Cluster
In the Canton of Zürich, almost eighty thousand people work in the creative industries sector, mainly in the sub-segments architecture, design, game design, music and press. Creative industries undoubtedly contribute to Zürich's leading international position in quality-of-life rankings, thanks in no small part to the rich diversity of Zürich's music, culture and gastronomy scenes, and the regularly held events.

A few Key Players: Zürich University of the Arts (ZHdK), F+F Schule für Kunst und Design, Disney Research Zürich, Swiss Game Developers Association, Swiss Society of Engineers and Architects (SIA), Design Biennale Zürich, Blickfang, Designgut, Kreislauf 345, m4music and neue Räume.

ICT Cluster

In the Canton of Zürich, approximately fifty thousand people work in more than five thousand ICT companies. The gross added value in the Canton of Zürich amounted to approximately CHF 11.2 billion in 2015. ICT specialists are employed in various areas, including in the financial, insurance and commerce sectors.

A few Key Players: ETH Zürich, ZHAW, eZuerich.ch, digitalswitzerland, Digital Festival Zürich (including HackZürich hackathon), Google Research, IBM Research, Ergon, Namics, Liip, Netcetera, Topsoft , Swiss ICT Award, SICTIC.

Life Sciences Cluster

The research-intensive development and production in the life-sciences cluster benefits from Zürich's broad academic base via the Federal Institute of Technology (ETH), the University of Zürich, the University Hospitals, and the Zürich University of Applied Sciences (ZHAW). The increasing momentum in this cluster is due to the spin-off activities stemming from the universities.

A few Key Players: BIO-TECHNOPARK® Schlieren-Zürich, Wyss Zürich, University Medicine Zürich, Life Science Zürich, Balgrist Campus, Competence Center Personalized Medicine in Zürich, Department of Health Sciences and Technology at ETH Zürich, ZHAW Life Sciences, Swiss Medtech, Swiss Biotech, Toolpoint for Lab Science, Swiss Healthcare Startups, Grow Wädenswil.

Cleantech Cluster

The thriving cleantech cluster in Zürich is based on Switzerland's reputation of tackling environmental challenges while providing sustainable, high-quality, environmentally friendly services in the urban environment The microclimate for startups is favorable with dedicated institutions such as Climate KIC Accelerator, EMPA and Club of Rome. Zürich companies played a pioneering role in the financing of cleantech activities.

A few Key Players: EMPA, NEST – Exploring the Future of Buildings, EMPA Move: EMPA's Future Mobility Demonstrator, Glatec, Climate KIC, Club of Rome, Agile Wind Power, Climeworks, Flisom, Southpole, Emerald Technology Ventures.

Aerospace Cluster

The aerospace cluster consists of the aviation, space flight and satellite navigation. Applications based on space infrastructure for telecommunication, earth and climate observation, precision timing, and navigation are a driving force behind all kinds of technologies.

A few Key Players: ESA Business Incubation Centre, Swiss Aerospace Cluster, Swiss Space Center, Marenco, Wingtra, Twingtec, Ruag Space.

Zürich finance cluster stands
second in Europe after London

The aerospace cluster consists
of the aviation, space flight and
satellite navigation

almost 80,000 people work
in the creative cluster

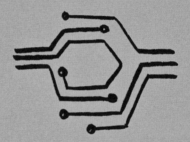

gross added value in 2015 was
around 11 billion CHF

life sciences cluster generates
a lot of spin-off activities

high reputation in tackling
environmental challenges

ups

[Name]
Balboa

[Elevator Pitch]

"We aim to become a lifestyle, a spirit, a global brand. We place the human body at the center of the experience, and connect body movement, mind and social activities."

[The Story]

Balboa was founded in 2014 by Erich Züger, who wanted to create a platform and hub for urban exchange by making a place where members could work out as well as hang out. He and cofounders Paco Savio and Timo Klein envision a network of places where interactions happen between young spirits of all ages and in all manner of combinations. Balboa has two boutique gyms thus far – Balboa Bar & Gym and Balboa im Viadukt – each with authentic interiors adapted to the characteristics of the building and the surrounding neighborhood.

The venues have dedicated training rooms for a variety of activities, from weightlifting to group classes like yoga, breakdance workouts and martial arts. There's also an in-house bar and cafe, easily viewable from the workout spaces and vice versa. The space was specifically designed to create this visual connection between the spaces. Even though the Balboa venues have been designed for workout functionality mixed with urban comfort chic, the company takes its social/workout manifesto to the streets and regularly hold workouts and group classes at unlikely public events, such as art fairs, and in coworking spaces, old industrial buildings and assorted retail shops.

[Funding History]

Bootstrap　　　Seed

Balboa started in a garage with enough of its own capital to create a company. It found interested investment parties within its client base to contribute to rounds A and B, totaling nearly CHF 2 million.

[Milestones]
- Developing our brand and name.
- Opening of the Garage, our laboratory where we could test our product and develop our spirit and brand.
- Setting up our first permanent location in the banking district and creating a cultural mix.
- Restructuring and analyzing our business in order to professionalize operations.

[Links] Web: **Web: balboamove.ch** Facebook: **balboamove** Twitter: **@balboamove** Instagram: **balboamove**

thirsty? hungry?

[Name]

Carbon Delta

[Elevator Pitch]

"We are a Zürich-based environmental fintech that analyzes climate change risks and helps banks and insurance companies understand and quantify these risks within their portfolio. Our Climate Value-at-Risk tool is designed for institutional investors."

[The Story]

It all started with the carbon bubble theory. Carbon Delta CEO and cofounder Oliver Marchand explains, "The theory posits that companies relying on fossil fuels are currently valued based on the available reserves. However, as the burning of these reserves would contribute to global warming (in excess of 2°C), their future use will likely be restricted, making them a stranded asset risk." While the theory gained some attention in financial markets, it was always clear to the founders of Carbon Delta that an even better risk tool was needed. Carbon Delta has developed software that uses big data to perform climate risk analysis of twenty-five thousand publicly listed companies. Furthermore, the team has built strategic partnerships with renowned institutions in the field of finance and climate science, including the German Potsdam Institute for Climate Impact Research.

"These partnerships allow us to access the necessary data to understand where and how companies operate," Oliver says. "When overlaying company-specific financial information with regulatory and climate data, it allows us to model the degree to which these companies will be affected by CO_2 prices, extreme weather events and cleantech innovations." Carbon Delta's data enables investors to stress-test their portfolios and, ultimately, to mitigate risks, increase return and meet regulatory requirements.

[Funding History]

Bootstrap

While Carbon Delta has been getting generous support from Climate-KIC (the largest public–private innovation partnership in Europe to focus on climate change), it has been financially independent from the beginning.

[Milestones]

- Successfully building a model for twenty-five thousand companies.
- Acquiring three large financial institutions as clients.
- Being announced as "Europe's Best Climate Venture of 2016" by Climate-KIC.
- Forming a strategic partnership with the Potsdam Institute for Climate Impact Research.

[Links] Web: **carbon-delta.com** Facebook: **CARBON.DELTA.AG** Twitter: **@carbondelta**

[Name]

CUTISS

[Elevator Pitch]

"We aim at significantly improving the life quality of patients worldwide who suffer from skin defects such as burns, scar revisions and tumor resections. We bioengineer customized skin that minimally scars after transplantation and which surgeons can apply using standard techniques."

[The Story]

CUTISS originally started in 2001 as a university research project between professors Martin Meuli and Ernst Reichmann with Dr Clemens Schiestl aimed at developing a new method of creating skin replacements from a patient's own cells. They commenced their first phase trials in 2014 and the success of the trials caught the research group off guard. They were left wondering how they could take the idea even further. CEO and cofounder Daniela Marino (who had joined the project in 2009) decided to turn the project into a product and created the company. "I got a business coach to help me with everything," she says. "So I basically went from being a post-doc scientist to an entrepreneur."

CUTISS gets a biopsy of a patient's skin shipped to its laboratory where cells from the skin sample are grown and turned into much larger skin grafts, until eventually the newly grown skin is ready to be transplanted onto the patient's body. The people who use CUTISS are divided into two main groups, Daniela says: "Acute and elective. Acute is for victims of burns or any kind of trauma, whereas elective is for someone who, for example, has disfiguring scars from old wounds or from previous surgeries. But our product can also be for gender reassignments, facial reconstruction surgery or basically anyone that has skin needs."

[Funding History]

Bootstrap   Seed

Initially self-funded, CUTISS received prize money from Venture and the W. A. De Vigier Foundation totaling CHF 170,000. It then received CHF 12 million in grants from FP7 EU, UZH and private sponsors, CHF 5 million from Wyss Zürich and CHF 1 million from the UZH Life Science Fund.

[Milestones]

- Successfully completing phase-one trials.
- Translating our product into GMP.
- Turning our project into a company.
- Getting Orphan Drug Designation for the treatment of burns from Swissmedic, EMA and FDA.

[Links]   Web: **cutiss.swiss** Facebook: **skingrafts**

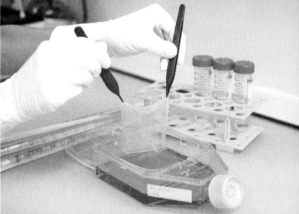

[Name]
ElectricFeel

[Elevator Pitch]
"We provide a platform to build, run and scale shared electric mobility services in cities. Our customers operate the services using our platform and have already enabled more than six million kilometers of clean mobility across Europe with e-bikes and e-scooters."

[The Story]
ElectricFeel was founded in 2012 as a spin-off from ETH Zürich, the Swiss Federal Institute of Technology. The founders, Moritz Meenen and Pratik Mukerji, have always been passionate about the genius of the bicycle, and they felt there was enormous potential in combining shared mobility architectures such as those that exist for bike-sharing but for e-scooters instead. Moritz says, "We wanted to develop a scalable technology that's both smart and ensures that sustainable business cases can be built around our platform." They decided to create a fleet-management software that they would use with partner suppliers of e-scooters. The platform makes sure that the e-scooters are available when and where people need them and also manages the scooter batteries intelligently.

ElectricFeel has a number of partnerships in other major cities aside from Zürich, enabling them to expand their service. Thus far, this includes Mainz, Barcelona, Madrid, Rome and Lisbon. With more than 1,500 e-scooters in service, Moritz is happy to see a positive impact being made. "It's amazing to see how you can find hundreds of these nice little e-scooters around the city. They don't stink, and they're silent, so you can even have a conversation while you're riding on them."

[Funding History]

Angel   External

As of 2016, the company has managed to raise a round of investment from some prominent Swiss investors, and this has gone towards accelerating their product and business development.

[Milestones]
- Developing a model with ETH Zürich to accurately predict how people use bike-sharing in real-time.
- Launching our station-based bike- and e-bike-sharing platform (including in the city of Mainz).
- Developing free-floating e-scooter-sharing, and launching with eCooltra, Europe's leading scooter-rental company.
- Expanding to Madrid, Rome and Lisbon, and becoming the largest e-scooter-sharing project.

[Links]   Web: electricfeel.com Facebook: electricfeelnow Twitter: @theelectricfeel

[Name]
Farmy

[Elevator Pitch]
"We're an online grocery market for ethical food. We bring regional and responsibly produced food products straight from the farm directly to your home."

[The Story]
Farmy was founded in 2014 by e-commerce professionals Tobias Schubert and Roman Hartmann. They wanted to combine their industry experience with their passion for local and sustainable food produce. Roman elaborates on their mission: "We provide a platform that cuts out the middleman in selling food produce. Consumers go to our website and choose what they want from over six thousand products, and each item can be linked back to a producer profile where you can find out where the item is coming from and who produced it. This creates transparency."

Transparency isn't the only benefit of ordering food through Farmy. "The produce comes straight from the producer to our warehouse, where it's packaged before being delivered to the consumer's door," Roman says, "so it's a lot fresher – up to three days fresher than the supermarkets." To top it off, Farmy use electric vehicles for their deliver operations. So far, Farmy has around six hundred producer profiles on their website. Their producers are carefully selected to be as close as possible, as shorter routes guarantee fresher food. Given that not all of the producers are so digitally savvy, Farmy also helps them with setting up their profile and marketing.

[Funding History]

Bootstrap   Seed   Angel   External

Farmy closed a seed round in 2014 with several business angels. This was followed by Series A in 2015 with Jucker Farm AG and a family office, Series B with Pistor AG in 2016, and Series C in 2017, with participation from Swiss politician Ruedi Noser and Fabio Borzatta. In total they have received CHF 10 million since launching.

[Milestones]
- Getting financing, which is not so easy in this industry.
- Getting a good understanding of our customer's needs.
- Learning how to acquire customers for an online food-industry model.
- Finding the right people for the management team.

[Links] Web: **farmy.ch** Facebook: **farmy.ch** Twitter: **@farmyCH** Instagram: **farmy_ch**

[Name] # ImagineCargo

[Elevator Pitch] *"Our mission is a total revolution in logistics. We're dramatically reducing the negative impact of deliveries in and between cities by creating an environmentally and socially responsible alternative to the conventional logistics networks."*

[The Story] ImagineCargo was started in 2014 by Nick Blake, who had the idea of building a sustainable, express network for logistics transport between cities using only bicycles and trains. Using this unique combination of transport ensures a better speed of delivery and up to 99 percent reduction in emissions. "Cycle couriers have a distinct advantage when delivering in cities," CEO Ville Heimgartner says. "They can deliver from A to B without the hindrance of things like traffic jams that conventional transporters get stuck in – and often contribute to." Intercity train routes provide the long-haul part of a delivery, while ImagineCargo's cycle couriers are on hand to deliver from the business to the train, and then from the train to the business at the other end.

The bike couriers operate on specialized, electrically assisted tricycles which come with different sized rear-compartments. These can comfortably transport items up to 2.2 meters in length and up to 300 kg. ImagineCargo is currently connecting the largest cities in Germany, Austria and Switzerland, and has plans to expand. Its vision is to have completely emission-free distribution of all goods in urban areas.

[Funding History]

Bootstrap   Seed

For the first few years, ImagineCargo was self-funded. In 2014, it won the Climate-KIC Competition with CHF 24,000 in prize money. It has recently become involved in a project with Engagement Migros, from whom it will receive funding over the course of three years.

[Milestones]
- Stopping same-day service in Austria due to ÖBBs discontinuing its package service on the trains (a brief spanner in the works).
- Establishing a subsidiary in Berlin and launching a same-day service in Germany.
- Shifting our focus from a same-day service to a city-logistics service.
- Signing our first major city-logistics customer in Switzerland.

[Links] Web: **imaginecargo.com** Facebook: **ImagineCargo** Twitter: **@ImagineCargo**

[Name] # modum.io

[Elevator Pitch] *"We combine IoT sensors with blockchain technology to provide data integrity for transactions involving physical products. We offer a passive monitoring solution to streamline the supply chain processes in many sectors."*

[The Story] Supply chain logistics are in the midst of a major shakeup: blockchain technology offers companies a secure and transparent method of ensuring authenticity and favorable shipment conditions for products. Moving ahead of the curve, modum.io, with their team of engineers, developers and designers, have applied blockchain and IoT technology to develop a global supply-chain solution. Their first product tackles the stringent regulatory requirements in the European pharma industry, which require temperature monitoring of all medicinal products in transit. The modum solution fits within existing last-mile logistics processes by pairing parcels with sensors that monitor conditions such as temperature while in transit. The data can be read by both the sender and receiver on smart devices.

The company was founded in 2016 after winning a number of competitions (including Kickstart Accelerator) and launching a number of regional and international pilot projects. According to Michael Taylor, modum's marketing and communications lead, the pilots were highly successful and yielded a wealth of insight from customers. With the validation that each of the successful pilots provided, modum confidently enters the market with its own sensor hardware in early 2018. The team thinks of their company as "blockchain enabling," and they are eager to develop an early market-driven use case and to pioneer new applications of blockchain technology in the global supply chain.

[Funding History]

Bootstrap

In September 2017, modum held a token sale to fund ongoing operations. The MOD Token was purchased by over four thousand crypto-investors, raising $US13.5 million (based on conversion rates at the time of the sale). The community established around the MOD Token has been fundamental in generating a strong support for modum's first product.

[Milestones]
- Winning Kickstart Accelerator's Future and Emerging Technologies Vertical in fall 2016.
- Completing three pilot projects with customers in Central Europe and the Middle East.
- Raising $13.5 million in an initial token sale in September 2017.
- Beginning mass production of modum's proprietary sensor technology in early 2018.

[Links]   Web: **modum.io** Twitter: **@modum_io**

[Name]
TestingTime

[Elevator Pitch]
"We're the world's largest online test-user recruitment platform for UX designers and market researchers."

[The Story]
Cofounder and CEO Reto Laemmler was previously VP of product management at Doodle until he decided to leave the company to create his own venture. "I saw a huge potential in the UX and user-testing market," he says, "but there was no fast and easy-to-use service for recruiting test users." He started TestingTime as a side project in 2014 with cofounder Oliver Ganz. It very quickly gained traction, and in 2015 they decided to incorporate it into a proper company. In the same year, they closed a substantial seed round and proved scalability across Europe.

TestingTime's customers are in the UX and market-research industries, and both markets are in need of participants for usability tests, interviews, focus groups, diary studies and surveys. TestingTime provides a pool of more than one hundred thousand test users from which their customers can order their desired target users for qualitative and quantitative user research online. Test users are acquired through online campaigns and referral mechanisms, and the smart rating system and predictive machine-learning algorithms ensure high-quality test users with a low no-show rate. TestingTime is currently used by large corporations across Europe such as UBS, Zalando, Microsoft and Accenture.

[Funding History]

Bootstrap   Seed

TestingTime was bootstrapped, and the team validated the business model using the lean startup principle. After incorporating in 2015, they closed a seed round of CHF 850,000 from Investiere.

[Milestones]
- Validating our business model using the lean startup principle.
- Closing a seed round.
- Proofing scalability outside Switzerland.
- Crossing the CHF 1 million annual-revenue mark.

[Name]
UrbanFarmers

[Elevator Pitch]
"The fresh produce revolution from the roof. We provide systems and solutions that enable enterprises to grow the freshest vegetables and fish in your city reliably, and on a large scale."

[The Story]
UrbanFarmers founder Roman Gaus wants to bring fresh produce to the rooftops with their unique, decentralized farming systems. He'd never considered himself the farming type, but he'd long been dissatisfied with widespread methods for producing and transporting fresh produce, often entailing lots of chemicals and mass transportation. "It didn't seem like the best solution for the consumer or the environment," Roman says, "and I felt that there needed to be more efficiency and sustainability in producing food, especially for what we'll require in the coming years."

In 2011, Roman discovered that he could combine the model of urban farming that he'd witnessed in the States with a closed-loop system of growing plants and fish called Aquaponics, which was developed by the Zürich University of Applied Sciences. In this innovative technology, the plants provide a natural filter for the water that the fish live in, and waste from the fish serves as a food source for the plants. Aquaponics uses 90 percent less water than conventional agriculture and requires no pesticides or antibiotics, making it 100 percent organic, all without soil and all year round. UrbanFarmers now have a flagship product of fully constructed farms, ready to be placed in any urban location, be it land, water, or on rooftops.

[Funding History]

External

UrbanFarmers have thus far made a total of CHF 10 million, with series A and B rounds with external funding from family, office and impact investors making up 50 percent. The other 50 percent was raised in project financing with real estate owners.

[Milestones]
- Incorporating the Aquaponics system from ZHAW in 2011.
- Constructing our pilot rooftop farm, LokDepot in 2011.
- Collaborating with Migros, the largest Swiss food retailer.
- Constructing UF de Schilde, the largest rooftop farm in the EU, in The Hague in 2016.

[Links]   Web: urbanfarmers.com Facebook: UrbanFarmers Twitter: @UrbanFarmersCH

[Name] # Wildbiene + Partner

[Elevator Pitch] *"We're multiplying mason bees with the help of our community to sustainably pollinate fruit orchards."*

[The Story] Without bee pollination, humanity would lose an abundance of foods such as apples, pears, mangoes and even coffee – and yet bee populations worldwide are in serious decline. Wildbiene + Partner aim to stop the decline by supplying BeeHomes in which you can keep bees as "pets" and help to increase their numbers. The idea is the brainchild of biologist Claudio Sedivy, who teamed up with Tom Strobl to create the company in 2013. The BeeHome is a shoebox-sized wooden box with a series of small elongated tubes that are used as nests by the bees. Once grown, the baby bees are sent back (inside their BeeHomes) to Wildbiene + Partner, who will prepare them for farmers to use in pollinating crops the following year. The BeeHome then goes back to the owner to start the breeding process all over again.

Wildbiene + Partner use mason bees, a type of wild bee that is much more efficient at pollinating than others and, as Claudio says, "They don't sting and are very safe to host on your balcony." Wildbiene + Partner is also available to make what it calls the BeeParadise: "We build gardens in private or public properties with native plants and bee-nesting structures to promote all kinds of solitary bees. These are also beautiful places for people to enjoy, and to learn all about bees."

[Funding History]

Bootstrap

Seed

Angel

Wildbiene + Partner placed first in the "Hub Fellowship for a Green Economy," winning CHF 42,000 in prize money. Additionally, it received CHF 30,000 from the Ernst E. Moppler foundation and, as of 2016, closed a Series A funding round of CHF 2.4 million with three angel investors.

[Milestones]
- Getting a fellowship with Impact Hub Zürich.
- Being featured on a famous Swiss TV show called Äschbacher.
- Making the connection with Richard Hollenstein (a well-respected farming consultant).
- Closing our Series A funding round.

[Links] Web: **wildbieneundpartner.ch** Facebook: **Wildbiene.und.Partner** Instagram: **wildbieneundpartner**

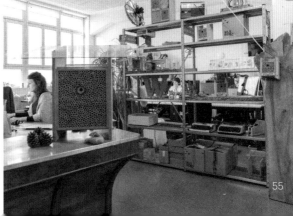

rams

- **Have a skilled team.**
  We want to see a diverse team with relevant skills
  to transform ideas to reality.

- **Minimum of two full-time team members.**
  To really let your startup take off, we need at least
  two people on board at all times.

- **Show commitment to the cause.**
  We are tackling a serious issue so we need passion
  towards making real change for the better.

- **Have a scalable service/product.**
  Climate change is a world issue. We want you to
  go big.

- **High level of innovativeness.**
  Big problems require big solutions.

[Name]

Climate-KIC Accelerator

[Elevator Pitch]

"We are Europe's largest cleantech accelerator supporting over two hundred climate-relevant startups a year."

[Sector]

Cleantech, greentech

[Description]

Climate-KIC is a Europe-wide initiative to address climate change through innovation. They have a number of country-specific programs tailored to incubate and accelerate startups from relevant fields. The Climate-KIC Accelerator in Zürich takes six to eighteen months to complete and is divided into three stages. The selection process involves putting calls out as well as scouting for potential participants, culminating in the final ten to twelve startups making a final pitch to judges for inclusion. The program takes no equity, and grant funding up to €95,000 can be given over the course of the program.

The first stage of the accelerator aims to help the startups develop their MVP and general business model. The startups are able to finalize their prototypes with valuable feedback from relevant industry professionals. There's also one-on-one mentoring and masterclass workshops, as well as boot camps and networking events that give the startups access to Climate-KIC's European network. It's at this first stage that each startup gets substantial financial support with a grant of €20,000.

As they say at Climate-KIC, "Technology startups seldom fail on technology; they fail on commercialization," so the second stage is focused on customer acquisition and traction, a critical stage for the validation of the business model. Now that the idea and prototype are firmly set in place, the startups are already working on getting their first customers, all the while getting continuous support from the coaches and mentors. Finally, the third stage of the accelerator focuses on the startups becoming investment-ready, so the teams get support in preparation for scaling up, pitching and negotiating with potential investors.

The Climate-KIC Accelerator runs not only in Zürich but also Berlin, Munich, Frankfurt, Vienna and fifteen other locations around Europe.

[Apply to]

climate-kic-dach.org/#apply

[Links]

Web: **climate-kic-dach.org** Facebook: **ClimateKIC** Twitter: **@ClimateKIC**

- **Build negotiation experience.**
  You'll be working with advisors and dealing with
  the stakeholders, VCs, angels and various funds.

- **Share common goals with your cofounders.**
  Fellow cofounders might have a different idea of
  timing, so you all need to be on the same page with
  your exit strategy.

- **Learn to communicate with external parties.**
  Investors are expecting you to be able to answer
  their questions about the exit and the steps involved.

- **Identify potential pitfalls.**
  Sometimes things don't always go as planned, so an
  agile mindset will help you cope with possible pitfalls
  and deal-breakers.

Exit Accelerator

[Name]

[Elevator Pitch] *"We're a grassroots, nonprofit organization that aims to boost startup and SME ecosystems by promoting awareness, trainings and exposure to exits. We help with exit preparation for mature startups, and assist in introductions, visibility and deal-flow for service providers, lawyers and M&A experts."*

[Sector] **Startup exits, mergers and acquisitions (M&A)**

[Description] There are many initiatives that support startups in their early growth stage, yet very few for later stage startups and even less with a focus on exits. Exit Accelerator fills this rather large void with their tailor-made approach for startups about to be released into the great business wilderness. Startups can easily get used to the warm cocoon of a nurturing program, but it's never too early to be thinking ahead to E-day.

Exit Accelerator operates on an ongoing basis rather than going down the fixed-time route of other programs, and the primary goal is to facilitate conversations about exits and the necessary strategies. There's a big emphasis on making startups aware of issues like the time, costs and risks involved in the exit process; the emotional impact of an exit for entrepreneurs; and what can be a deal killer. Even though the aim is to guide individual startups towards a successful exit, the accelerator looks at the bigger picture in terms of how the Swiss startup ecosystem can benefit, such as by increasing investment flow to Switzerland. Exit Accelerator acknowledges the huge value in learning from previous experiences, and there's ample opportunity for startups to engage fellow entrepreneurs and industry experts and to learn from past successes and failures.

A common sentence heard in any startup scene is: "I wish I knew then what I know now." Exit Accelerator makes sure that there are plenty of industry experts to share their experiences and answer any burning questions that participants might have. Exit Accelerator offers a range of options for startups and founders to connect with relevant industry professionals such as one-on-one calls during business hours, conferences and networking events. The program also offers workshops, networking/spotlighting Swiss opportunities to foreign investors, awareness and education for founders, and assistance establishing an M&A network. The accelerator is active all over Switzerland.

[Apply to] ask@exitaccelerator.com

[Links] Web: **exitaccelerator.com** Facebook: **ExitAccelerator** Twitter: **@exitaccelerator**

- At least two founders of the team are ready to go full time.
  No time will be wasted in getting you ready, so at least two of you should be committed to going full time on the venture.

- Already identified the business problem and ready to verify.
  Your idea should be clear in terms of what customer problems it addresses and what the solution will be.

- Meets the business topic related to the sector.
  Your idea should be related to fintech, insurtech or regtech and solve a problem for the industry and/or customers (B2B or B2C).

- Have a team with experience.
  For best success, bring a team with some history together, who fit together as a unit.

F10 Incubator & Accelerator

[Name]

[Elevator Pitch] *"The F10 Incubator & Accelerator is a non-profit organization dedicated to helping startups turn their ideas into successful companies, and all without taking equity."*

[Sector] **Fintech, insurtech, regtech**

[Description] F10 offers three different components in its accelerator/incubator, with the main program being Prototype to Product (P2). It also offers the once-a-year Idea to Prototype (P1), which is a forty-eight-hour Thinking Idea Boot Camp that aims to turn ideas into valid prototypes. They also offer Product to Market (P3), which isn't a program per se but more of a means of facilitating collaboration between F10 corporate partners and startups to help build PoCs and network.

The P2 program takes place over the course of six months and is divided into five different units with workshops and lectures. These are 1) Vision, Team and Strategy; 2) Business, Product and Technology; 3) Marketing and Sales; 4) Legal, Regulations and Funding; and 5) Demo Day and Graduation. The program commences with organizers and startups agreeing on what milestones should be achieved. During the program, there will be three different assessments to check that the startups have reached their milestones; if not, they will not be able to continue. The first milestone is to identify a business problem and its solution, which must be achieved within the first three months. The second milestone is creating the MVP, and the third is being ready to receive seed investment.

Each participating team is given office space in the heart of Zürich city center, but it should be pointed out that not all team members need to make the move, as long as the startup has one representative based there. For international startups not already in Zürich, there can be up to CHF 15,000 awarded for expenses while away from home, as long as the milestones have been reached. The F10 Incubator & Accelerator has an extensive global network of banks, regulators, angels and VCs for startups to get acquainted with, as well as internationally renowned mentors and coaches who will be on hand to support and guide the startups all along the way.

[Apply to] f10.ch/startup-program/#p2

- **Be in Switzerland.**
  To be eligible for the Innosuisse's Start-up Coaching and Training programs, entrepreneurs need be based in Switzerland or intend to create a business based in the country.

- **Have an innovative business idea in science or technology that can be protected.**
  The degree of innovation of your business idea will be evaluated against the current state of the market, as well as its competitiveness, and must have the potential to be protected.

- **Have potential to scale and grow.**
  The startup's performance to date and its growth potential are reviewed. If an idea or business is not scalable, chances are slim that it will be accepted into the program.

- **Be open to input.**
  The founders will be assessed for their commitment to implementing the idea and their openness to receiving feedback.

[Name]
Innosuisse Start-up Coaching and Training

[Elevator Pitch]
"We accompany young entrepreneurs throughout the entire spectrum of their business development – from igniting the initial entrepreneurial spark all the way to business growth."

[Sector]
Science, technology, innovation

[Description]
Innosuisse's Start-up Coaching and Training programs are designed to support science- and technology-based entrepreneurs who intend to create a business based in Switzerland or have already founded one in the country. Both programs play a role in Innosuisse's broader mission to promote innovation in Switzerland. To apply for either program, entrepreneurs or startups need to complete an online application.

The Start-up Training program offers four modules to help budding entrepreneurs develop their business idea, set up a company and implement a strategy for growth. The focus here is more on people who have an innovative business idea and need guidance on making it a reality, or entrepreneurs who are in the process of founding a company. There are four separate training and development modules to choose from, and all courses are taught by experienced entrepreneurs and executed by mandated providers.

On the Start-up Coaching front, there are three programs available depending on the stage of the idea or business. The programs offer selected applicants personalized coaching to facilitate growth through a voucher with financial credit that can be used to redeem services from a selected pool of Innosuisse-approved coaches. First, there's an Initial Coaching program that offers a voucher worth up to CHF 5,000 and is for entrepreneurs who have a business idea and need expert advice on its feasibility and marketability. In the Core Coaching program, the economic viability of a business idea is further evaluated, and startups receive customized support worth up to CHF 50,000 to reach milestones in their business plan. Here, coaching and workshops tackle topics that range from advice on business model optimization and product development to organization structure and go-to-market strategies. Finally, the Scale-Up Coaching program will be available to high-growth potential enterprises in 2018. It aims to provide a significant boost in scaling and international expansion plans with a voucher worth up to CHF 75,000.

[Apply to]
www.innosuisse.ch

[Links]
Web: innosuisse.ch Facebook: Innosuisse Twitter: @_Innosuisse

- **Be at MVP point.**
  You should already have traction with your product/service.

- **Have a convincing pitch.**
  We want to see an appealing value proposition with lots of potential.

- **Show ambition.**
  Your startup should be ambitious, with a well-thought-out road map of where you want to go.

- **Be in Zürich.**
  Your startup should be ready to stay, live and work in Zürich for the program's duration.

Kickstart Accelerator

[Name]

[Elevator Pitch]

"We are one of Europe's largest zero-equity, multicorporate accelerators. Startups are provided with seed funding, direct access to leading corporate partners, investors, mentors and the chance to secure a proof of concept with the corporate partners."

[Sector]

Food, fintech, robotic and intelligent systems, and smart cities

[Description]

Kickstart Accelerator is an initiative of Impact Hub Zürich that is supported by digitalswitzerland and different leading organizations from the public and private sector in Switzerland. It's one of Europe's largest zero-equity, multicorporate accelerators and its aim is to put the Swiss innovation ecosystem on the global map of entrepreneurship. For several weeks, startups from all over the world come to Zürich to receive high-quality support to develop their businesses. The program is open to local and international startups with a focus on fintech, food and smart cities, though any startup with a disruptive idea is encouraged to apply. Kickstart Accelerator is particularly keen on startups that implement deep technologies, such as blockchain, AI, data mining, machine learning, IoT and computer vision, into their business idea. Participants each receive up to CHF 15,000 in seed funding and have the chance to get additional grants during the program.

Each startup is connected with a mentor who shares insights from their own experience, answers any questions, and helps them to leverage networks. Kickstart Accelerator encourages a long-lasting relationship between the mentor and startup that goes beyond the program's conclusion. Startups get great opportunities to have one-on-one sessions with a large number of industry experts on topics like business and product development, marketing and sales, fundraising, and more. Additionally, the program provides access to a wide range of leading corporate partners and investors who impart their wisdom and assist with developing PoC and other possible projects. During the program, the startups work at the Kraftwerk coworking space right in the heart of Zürich, and international startups are given help in finding local accommodation.

Regular community-building events are held at the coworking space and elsewhere in the Zürich city center with the aim of connecting startups with Switzerland's culture and innovation ecosphere. At the end of the program, on demo day, startups pitch to a wide audience of investors, executives and other key players.

[Apply to]

kickstart-accelerator.com/apply

[Links]

Web: kickstart-accelerator.com Facebook: KickstartAccelerator Twitter: @ks_accelerator

- **A desire for deep learning and leadership ambitions.**
  We're looking for people who have leadership
  ambitions, an entrepreneurial appetite and a desire
  for both deep learning and personal transformation.

- **Commitment.**
  To participate in this program, you should have the
  time, space and resources to do so.

- **No set project.**
  You will cocreate a venture, so it's important that you
  don't come with a fixed idea.

- **Have English fluency.**
  In order to get the most out of networking and coworking possibilities, you'll need to understand English.

[Name]
STRIDE

[Elevator Pitch]
"We support professionals, career-shifters and game-changers to engage in a deep process where entrepreneurial action with a purpose and self-development strengthen each other."

[Sector]
Education

[Description]
STRIDE, which calls itself the "unSchool for Entrepreneurial Leadership," is a spinoff from Impact Hub Zürich. The coordinators have set up a learning center with a radically different approach to learning, designed especially for potential entrepreneurial leaders looking for both meaning and purpose. The "unschool" is committed to personalizing the learning experience and helping to model the learning path according to the individual's interests and needs. STRIDE offers a few different learning path options such as Career Compass (one-on-one career guidance consultations) and STRIDE Labs (one-and-a-half day topical learning courses).

The main STRIDE course is the uDEL (unDiploma in Entrepreneurial Leadership), which is split into two different paths, STRIDE Core and STRIDE Deep, and takes place over eight months. STRIDE Core covers the whole spectrum of personal development, as well as collaboration and venture building. As part of the program, participants are required to set their individual learning outcomes by creating a learning contract, where they outline what they wish to focus on during the program. There are coaches on hand to help at every step, guiding and assisting to make sure these outcomes are achieved. The main component of the uDEL is the "build-ups," which are monthly, intensive workshops that get participants to engage with each other and workshop their ideas and ventures.

Additionally, there are three offsite build-up sessions that take place for up to nine days, one in Berlin and the other two in the Swiss mountains, to really freshen things up. STRIDE also organizes regular events and coworking days where the ventures have a chance to get to know each other and network with the participating uDEL experts. STRIDE Deep is the same but with extras, such as three years' extended access to STRIDE Labs, full Impact Hub Zürich Nomad memberships and direct access to pursue an MBA at Business School Lausanne with the possibility to transfer learning credits from uDEL.

[Apply to]
stride-learning.ch/apply-now

[Links]
Web: **stride-learning.ch** Facebook: **stridelearning** Twitter: **@StrideLearning**

- **Have a solid and well-balanced team.**
  We want a well-represented team with specialists in
  all relevant areas and with a good male:female ratio.

- **Have a realistic market expectation.**
  We see too many startups fail because of unrealistic
  expectations, so we want you to be grounded.

- **Be a highly scalable business model.**
  We want you to be realistic, but we also want to see
  an idea that can be taken globally.

- **Have intellectual property.**
  We don't want to be dealing with copycat products.

[Name]
Swiss Startup Factory

[Elevator Pitch]
"We're the only fully privately financed and independent startup accelerator in Switzerland. However, we're not a traditional accelerator program but more a business-driven execution platform for the most promising startup teams of Switzerland."

[Sector]
ICT, fintech and more

[Description]
Swiss Startup Factory is an independent startup accelerator that has the goal of building successful startups in both the ICT and fintech sectors, though other verticals are considered as well. Each year, up to twenty of the most talented startups are accepted into the program, which has the ambitious aim of getting each startup from idea to market within three months. Within the framework of a tailor-made program, the young entrepreneurs complete three main milestones to prepare them for the founding of their businesses: they must create an effective business model, complete a basic prototype ready to demonstrate, and show their MVP at a pitch event.

The organizers are very hands-on and keep close, daily contact to make sure that the team's passion for their idea remains but also stays within the confines of realistic goals. There are several input sessions throughout the program to align necessary expert advice with the guidance needed at each point. Aside from access to a unique network platform of over eighty investors, corporates, mentors and academics, the Swiss Startup Factory is also affiliated with one of the most active early-stage startup investors in the country, the Swiss Startup Group.

The startups are each given their own office space to base operations from, but the program also includes survival days where participants go out into nature to take part in team-building exercises. As the program deals predominantly with later-stage startups, there's a big emphasis on making a tight-knit team to drive the company forward. Milestones are organized as events where the startups go before a jury of ten to present their progress, with the jury deciding whether they get to move forward in the program. These events each conclude with a celebration dinner and a special guest speaker from the Zürich startup ecosphere who shares their thoughts and experiences. There is also the chance to mingle and network with influential industry figures.

[Apply to]
ssuf.typeform.com/to/S8kShi

[Links]
Web: **swissstartupfactory.com** Facebook: **SwissStartUpFactory** Twitter: **@s_s_uf** Instagram: **ssuf_ch**

-   **Be in Switzerland.**
    The Swisscom StartUp Challenge is committed to contributing to the Swiss tech and entrepreneurial ecosystem, so the startup must be based in Switzerland.

-   **Communicate why your startup is a good fit.**
    The program offers access to Swisscom's network, so startups with products or services that have a connection to the telecommunications company would likely get more from it.

-   **Have a top-notch pitch deck.**
    Your pitch deck should include all relevant information about your startup, its needs and goals.

-   **Be clear about what you want to achieve during the program.**
    The more precise entrepreneurs can be about what they want to achieve during the program, the more the program can be tailored to help them succeed.

[Name]

Swisscom StartUp Challenge

[Elevator Pitch]

"We're looking for the five best startups in Switzerland. We offer winners a unique opportunity to receive pitch training and participate in a tailored acceleration program in Silicon Valley where they will learn from top entrepreneurs and VCs."

[Sector]

ICT, mobile, high tech

[Description]

Once a year, the Swisscom StartUp Challenge flies five innovative Swiss startups to Silicon Valley for a customized week-long business acceleration program where they learn from top entrepreneurs, business leaders, VCs and tech companies. Swisscom, a major telecom company in Switzerland with headquarters in Bern, offers the winners sales and marketing workshops, pitch training, and the opportunity to network with key players in Silicon Valley's tech scene, all part of a program tailored to help them meet their business objectives. Startups also receive ongoing regular access to Swisscom's network of mentors and experts and will be considered for a business collaboration with Swisscom and/or investment by Swisscom Ventures.

Since 2013, the Swisscom StartUp Challenge has received over 650 applications and selected startups have received CHF 73 million from Swisscom Ventures and other investors. A call for submissions usually begins in early spring. It's open to startups at any stage – from early stage through mature extension stage – and to tech startups in any sector, from mobile and smart cities to artificial intelligence and fintech. Since the Swisscom StartUp Challenge is committed to contributing to the Swiss tech and entrepreneurial ecosystem, the main requirement is that the startup be based in Switzerland. Although not necessary, it helps if a startup's product or service has a connection to Swisscom and its business.

To apply, startups must submit a pitch deck and fill out an online form. It's important to clearly outline why you're a good fit for the accelerator program, what you hope to achieve in Silicon Valley, and where you see your startup in the future. After applications are evaluated, ten finalists are selected and invited to pitch at an event in front of a jury made up of members of the Swisscom Group Executive Board, Swisscom Ventures and external investors and business angels. Each startup receives feedback, and then five are announced as winners.

[Apply to]

swisscom.ch/en/business/start-up/programs/swisscom-startup-challenge

[Links]

Web: **swisscom.ch/startup** Facebook: **Swisscom.Business** Twitter: **@SwisscomStartUp**

ces

BlueLion Incubator

[Name]

[Address] Sihlquai 125, 8005 Zürich

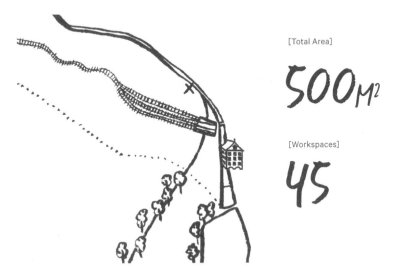

[Total Area]

500m²

[Workspaces]

45

[The Story] "We like to think of ourselves as a playground for tech startups," says Giada Polini, the BlueLion community and communications manager. The BlueLion Incubator, which opened in early 2017, places their prime focus on building community, not only between the startups that pull up a desk but also within corporations, through their innovative intrapreneurship program that enables corporate collaboration. BlueLion as a foundation has existed since 2012 when it was founded by the City of Zürich, ETH, UZH, Swisscom, ZKB, Stiftung Effort and Christian Wenger. The mission was, as it is now, to help ICT and cleantech startups grow sustainably and to spread innovation throughout the Swiss ecosystem.

The incubator space is only a few minutes' walk away from Zürich Central Station and has a plethora of cafés, restaurants and bars nearby. Though small, it packs in a lot: there's no shortage of meeting rooms and working spaces, and it also offers a large open area for community events and gatherings. The BlueLion Incubator also provides a range of services, such as pitch training, legal support, design prototyping and even admin support, but they make a point of offering customized packages, depending on the startup and their individual needs. "Even though there are many different mindsets operating at BlueLion, we're united in our goal to make an impact," says Giada.

[Links] Web: bluelion.ch Facebook: BlueLionIncubator Twitter: @BlueLionZurich

Face of the Space:

Giada Polini is a Swiss-Italian graphic designer who holds a fluid position at BlueLion, with roles ranging from graphic designer and communications manager to event organizer. She's been nicknamed the Chief of Happiness, as her job is to make sure that everyone working at or with BlueLion has a good time while doing it.

Live und in Farbe

Videokonferenz

In unserem Workshop-Raum steht Ihnen eine Videokonferenzanlage zur Verfügung. Mit zwei Bildschirmen, Tontechnik und einer Kamera überbrücken Sie die räumliche Distanz zu Ihren Gesprächspartnern.

[Name] # Büro Züri

[Address] Bahnhofstraße 9, 8001 Zürich

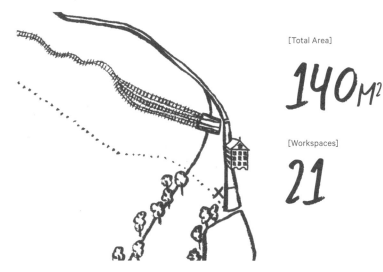

[Total Area]

140M²

[Workspaces]

21

[The Story] Büro Züri is provided free to the public by Zürcher Kantonalbank, the third largest bank in Switzerland. Founded in 1870 as the "bank of the citizens of Zürich," it's made a long and successful tradition of providing financial services and assistance to the locals. The cozy Büro Züri space was opened in 2015 as part of the newly renovated bank headquarters. "It's a coworking space in the heart of the financial district, open to all people," says Susanna von Känel, lead for the space. Any guest can reserve time in the space to study, work on an idea or grow their business.

Word has spread quickly, and the space now caters to a diverse mix of guests from the banking, tech and creative industries, as well as students. The fresh, modern and high-quality decor gives it a professional feel, which supports the image of local business people who use the space for work and meetings. There are also regular networking events and monthly breakfast gatherings with agendas driven by guests. "We always ask our guests what they want," Susanna says. During opening hours, there's always a community manager present to help, and free beverages and biscuits are available to maintain workers' energy levels. Büro Züri is easily accessible on the ground floor and is only a short walk from the northern tip of Lake Zürich.

[Links] Web: **buero-zueri.ch**

Face of the Space:
Susanna von Känel is responsible for Büro Züri's community curation and for the development of the space. She works for the bank, has studied economics and holds a degree in art education, which gives her the perfect combination of experience to provide an efficient, rational and creative space all in one.

[Name] # daycrunch

[Address]   Limmatquai 4, 8001 Zürich

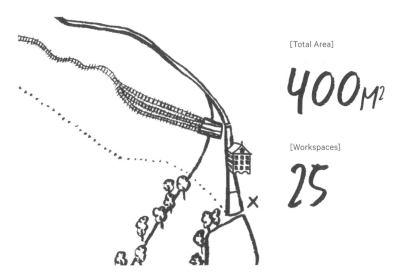

[Total Area]

400M²

[Workspaces]

25

[The Story]   The idea for daycrunch came to Vishal Mallick and his cofounders in 2013 when they realized that high-value office space was often left empty while landlords sought their next long-term tenant. The daycrunch solution puts the vacant offices back to work as smaller, configurable workspace layouts for short- to medium-term periods. The vision is to run these spaces within a multitude of buildings "using digitalization to change how society consumes space," says Vishal. The company behind daycrunch, Performance Buildings Ltd, created the technical platform that enables the rental process and connects all parties. daycrunch currently operates six locations – three in Zürich and three in other cities in Switzerland – with more opening in the coming months.

These self-service workspaces (which are usually 400 m² or larger) serve a wide range of customers, including corporate users, event organizers, startups and freelancers. Having teamed up with a furniture provider, daycrunch furnishes all the spaces with high-quality, designer office equipment. To ensure rates stay affordable, it uses no onsite staff: the platform is fully automated, enabling customers to book a space, unlock the door via a smartphone app, and come and go without additional human intervention. The company also limits its marketing and overhead spending, an approach that's working well: awareness of daycrunch has grown through word-of-mouth. By deliberately having no social media presence, daycrunch sees itself as a secret gem waiting to be found.

[Links]   Web: **daycrun.ch**

Face of the Space:

Vishal Mallick is a cofounder for daycrunch and leads Performance Buildings Ltd, the company behind the idea. A mechanical engineer by training, Vishal is now an entrepreneur fascinated by the opportunities and benefits of bringing digitization into the physical world. He is a man who wants to redefine offices for the twenty-first century.

[Name] # FabLab Zürich

[Address] Zimmerlistraße 6, 8004 Zürich

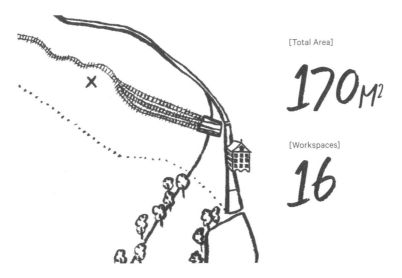

[Total Area]

170m²

[Workspaces]

16

[The Story] FabLab Zürich is one of more than one thousand FabLabs sprinkled around the world. The first FabLab was founded at the Massachusetts Institute of Technology (MIT) back in 2001, but since then it has become a movement and grown beyond the US. It provides not only a range of rapid-prototyping tools but also the education to get the most out of the machines. "The aim of a FabLab is to give its members low-threshold access to modern digital fabrication technologies," says Thomas Amberg, a lab manager at FabLab Zürich. "The FabLab is open to all makers, amateurs and professionals alike." Even neighbors and families with young children come along to create.

As part of FabLab's community-building modus operandi, there are regular workshops and events for learning and networking. Even though FabLab encourages creativity for fun, it also welcomes budding entrepreneurs and inventors to join the association so they can work on their ideas and develop prototypes for mass production at a later stage. At FabLab Zürich, members have a range of impressive equipment at their disposal, including 3D printers, laser cutters, CNC machines, knitting machines, plotters and woodworking tools.

[Links]   Web: **zurich.fablab.ch** Facebook: **fablabzurich** Twitter: **@fablabzurich**

Face of the Space:

Thomas Amberg is a maker and software engineer, the founder of Yaler.net, and an organizer of the IoT Meetup and a Maker Faire in Zürich. He's also a regular at the MechArtLab hackerspace and FabLab Zürich, where he volunteers as a lab manager and a member of the board.

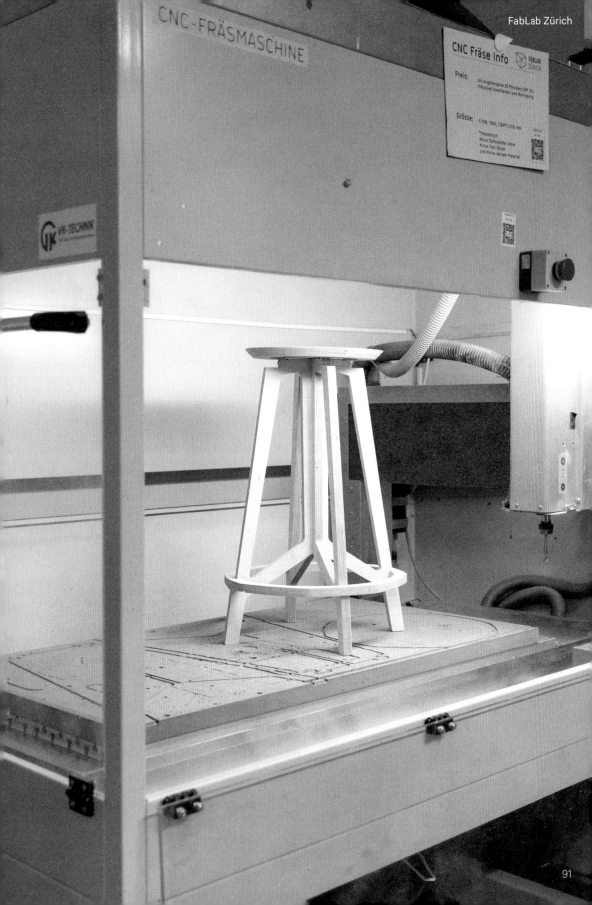

[Name] # Impact Hub Zürich

[Address]   Sihlquai 131, 8005 Zürich

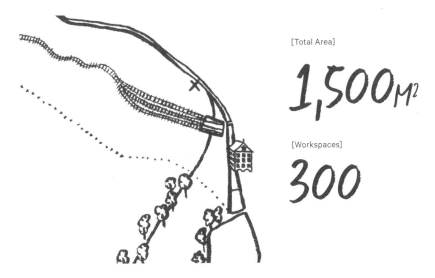

[Total Area]

1,500m²

[Workspaces]

300

[The Story]   Impact Hub is a network of over one hundred community and coworking spaces in locations around the globe, including São Paolo, Singapore, Johannesburg and San Francisco. Impact Hub Zürich's Colab location, the newest addition to the Zürich chapter, is housed in an old but beautifully retained brick building, which was formerly a factory for chemicals and lighting material. The five-floor building is bright and open, and every nook and cranny has been put to good use in the most stylish way possible. "The coworking space is an entirely open plan," says Dr. Christoph Birkholz, the managing director, "so the innovative spirit can fly around unhindered and the community can collaborate without walls or barriers." There are also many meeting rooms to choose from with capacity ranging from four to thirty in the stunning Loft Corner and Community Salon. The in-house cafe provides refreshments and is also available for catering.

The "MakerZpace" provides a range of machines, such as 3D printers and mini CNC cutters, for getting those prototypes up to scratch, and there's also a secluded area for companies to work on confidential prototypes. Impact Hub offers everything from a fixed resident desk to an easily obtainable club membership that gives access to not only other Impact Hub locations in Zürich and Switzerland but also all other Impact Hubs worldwide.

Face of the Space:

Dr. Christoph Birkholz is an entrepreneur based in Zürich. He is a cofounder and managing director of Impact Hub Zürich as well as inyova.com. He also cofounded Kickstart Accelerator, Viaduct Ventures and the Global Impact Hub Fellowship.

[Name] # Kraftwerk

[Address] Seinaustrasse 25, 8001 Zürich

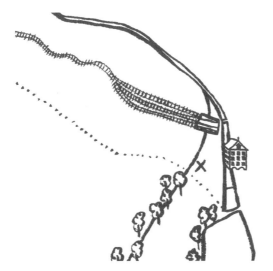

[Total Area]

1,400m²

[Workspaces]

200

[The Story] As a coworking space, Kraftwerk, which is affiliated with Impact Hub, is in a class of its own. It occupies the former power station of Zürich, and remnants of its past incarnation have been purposely left to give the space a very distinctive and almost museum-like flavor. There are two distinct parts of Kraftwerk separated by a large event space. On one side is the old "Command Room," which now serves as a meeting room. It has been lovingly kept as it once was, with its array of instruments and voltage meters from days gone by. Perhaps unsurprisingly, it's the most popular spot in the building to conduct business. Another striking part of Kraftwerk is the "Base Camp," a smartly arranged stack of shipping containers that have been refashioned into modern offices. The huge basement also offers ample working space.

Head curator Georgios Kontoleon says that Kraftwerk serves as a cross-corporation innovation space. "With this space, we're enabling partnerships between startups and more established companies in order to drive innovation and help foster the amazing talent we have in Zürich." The building also recently opened the Kraftwerk Cafe, which is a popular place for startups and the public alike.

[Links] Web: kraftwerk.host Facebook: KraftwerkZH Twitter: @KraftwerkZH

Face of the Space:

Georgios Kontoleon is a cofounder of Impact Hub Zürich and the software company Panter AG, where he's a member of the management team. He has a background in management and software engineering. He formerly initiated Colab Zürich and led the construction of the new Impact Hub Zürich locations Kraftwerk and Sihlquai.

[Name] # Rocket Hub

[Address]   Building STE, Stampfenbachstrasse 52/56, 8006 Zürich

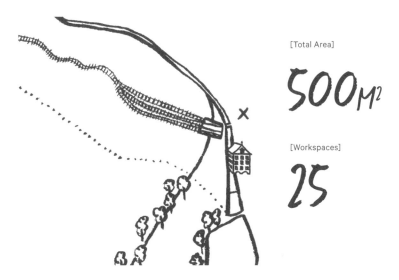

[Total Area]

500M²

[Workspaces]

25

[The Story]   Rocket Hub, run by the ETH Entrepreneur Club, was founded in 2015 on the campus of ETH Zürich University in what originally resembled more of a student house. By 2017, operations were moved to a fully modern, three-floor building renovated by ETH, just five minutes away from the original HQ and only two hundred meters from the central train station. Lida Vadakumchery, vice president of operations, explains that they're going for a vibrant and fun atmosphere where the creative juices can get flowing. "Alongside the working spaces and meeting rooms, there is a creative space with lots of color and sofas, and we get the tech startups to donate their broken robots to decorate the walls with." The creative space is also used for events such as Fuckup Nights and Startup Speed Dating.

Although the primary focus is on students, Rocket Hub opens its doors to anyone who wants to delve into entrepreneurship or who has a creative mindset. Even if you don't yet have fully formed ideas, the Rocket Hub community are there to help with advice or to exchange ideas or just share a drink. In addition to all the coffee one could want, there's also a restaurant situated on the ground floor.

[Links]   Web: **entrepreneur-club.org/rockethub** Facebook: **ETHEntrepreneurClub** Twitter: **@ec_zurich**

Face of the Space:

Lida Vadakumchery, vice president of operations at the ETH Entrepreneur Club, is in charge of managing the club's headquarters and coworking space, Rocket Hub. She's committed to connecting and hosting multidisciplinary teams and creating the perfect environment and opportunities to facilitate innovation, collaboration and creativity.

[Name] # Spaces Bleicherweg

[Address] Bleicherweg 10, 8002 Zürich

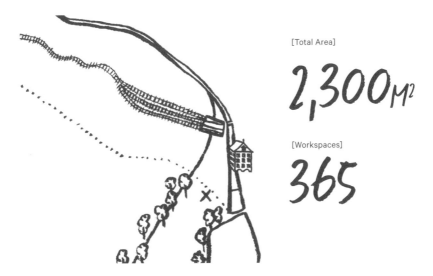

[Total Area]

2,300M²

[Workspaces]

365

[The Story] Spaces Bleicherweg is yet another chapter in this company's worldwide network of coworking spaces originally established in Amsterdam. The Spaces concept is to provide an inspiring but informal place to develop ideas and build businesses. It offers a relaxed alternative to the more office-like environments of other coworking options. In keeping with its approach of providing an open and friendly environment, the Zürich location has a number of options for startups from more closed off work stations to open-plan spaces for those who prefer a more collaborative environment, the sharing of ideas and friendly chats with passersby.

There are very flexible options for where you work and for how long you remain there. "Business arrangements can change rapidly, so we make our contracts flexible to reflect this," says Dzenana Medunjanin, the area manager. "You'll never have to sign your life away." Spaces Bleicherweg is located right in the heart of the action with a plethora of shopping and eating nearby but still close to the picturesque confines of Lake Zürich and Paradeplatz.

Face of the Space:
Dzenana Medunjanin is a five-year
ambassador for the Spaces company and
the area manager for the Zürich chapter.
She was in the ICT department in the original
Spaces in Amsterdam, and is a big believer
that clear communication is key to teamwork
and the growth of any organization.

[Name] # startup space

[Address]   Wiesenstraße 5, 8952 Schlieren-Zürich

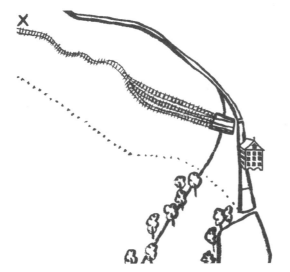

[Total Area]

1,500M²

[Workspaces]

100

[The Story]   In the district of Schlieren, on the outskirts of greater Zürich, startup space is housed in the modern confines of the Sony building, right next door to the Schlieren train station (with its abundant connections to the Zürich city center). The space is run by the IFJ (Institute for Young Entrepreneurs), who founded the space in 2016 in close cooperation with the city of Schlieren. The startup space comes with a diverse range of options for coworking, such as a seminar room with a 120-person capacity, as well as a number of networking zones, meeting spaces, an indoor lounge, a creation corner and, to top it all off, a spacious sun terrace. There's also in-house catering available, a number of coffee stations and snack machines.

The space provides extensive support for startups and entrepreneurs. "We offer a number of initiatives for free, such as an incorporation service, courses, an online business plan software, and an accounting solution to get you on your feet," says CEO Simon May. Additionally, there are two integrated spaces: the Coworking Limmattal area has lockable workstations and is run by Stadt Schlieren, and PostFinance offers six workplaces for nominated startups to use for up to six months at no cost.

[Links]   Web: **ifj.ch** Facebook: **IFJ.CH** Twitter: **@ifj_ch**

Face of the Space:
Simon May studied economics and holds an executive MBA. He's a member of the executive board of the IFJ and has been working in the Swiss startup scene since 2003. He's also a lecturer at the University of Applied Sciences St. Gallen in entrepreneurship, and a speaker at events in Switzerland and abroad.

[Name] # Technopark Zürich

[Address] Technoparkstraße 1, 8005 Zürich

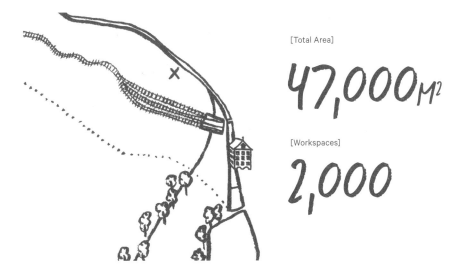

[Total Area]

47,000m²

[Workspaces]

2,000

[The Story] Technopark Zürich was established twenty-five years ago and was the first place for tech startups to set up their operations. Nowadays, the huge space takes in not only startups but also more mature companies. For that reason, there's a focus on providing individual office spaces. Team leader of foundation affairs Matthias Hölling explains that even though the spaces are more segregated, startups need not feel alone in their endeavors. "We regularly go around and talk to the companies to see if they have issues or need help, and we have an on-call advisory board to offer support when needed."

As the name implies, Technopark Zürich is a place for companies that are working on various technologies to hone their product or service. The building is equipped with a large self-service restaurant for the lunch crowd as well as a cafe for when you need to kickstart your brain with caffeine. There's a large array of different-sized meeting rooms available, as well as what Mathias likes to refer to as a "spillover work space" for excess company employees who might be visiting from abroad, for example. Technopark Zürich hosts various events throughout the year. These are predominantly informal networking breakfasts for the resident companies but are sometimes open to external companies as well.

[Links] Web: technopark.ch Facebook: technoparkzuerich Twitter: @technopark_zh

Face of the Space:

Matthias is an electrical engineer who has been in the local startup-up scene for more than ten years. He was responsible for supporting spin-off companies of ETH Zürich before joining Technopark Zürich. Apart from his coaching experience for startups, he has considerable know-how in intellectual property and IT management.

Patrick-Giorgio Baumberger / Raiffeisen Switzerland RAI Lab

President of the Swiss Fintech Innovations Association

Patrick Baumberger has been at the cutting edge of the Swiss fintech scene for nearly a decade now. He founded two startups himself focusing on mobile payments and new media, and served as vice president of Swiss Fintech Innovations SFTI. As Raiffeisen Switzerland's president of the Swiss Fintech Innovations Association, he helps foster new fintech businesses and integrate their products into the bank's services.

One of the biggest problems a new business faces is finding the resources to reach the market. When you're developing your business, you don't just need money to develop your product and pay your staff, you also need enough cash on hand to get your product to customers, whether that means setting up a physical supply chain or developing and releasing an app. And those needs can add up.

"When you're a startup, even when you've developed a solution, you need to find your customer," says Patrick. "It's essential that you have enough resources to distribute and test your product, and to grow your company when it's ready."

So how can your business get the funding that it needs? It might sound counterintuitive, but sometimes the best way to attract the kind of investment that will get your product to market is to just take it to market – even if it's not ready. Going to market early will let you refine your product as quickly as possible and make changes where necessary. A better product-market fit and value proposition will make you more attractive to investors, and you might even generate revenue on your own, extending your runway further.

"I know a lot of startups that aren't confident enough in their solutions to enter the market, but startups need to test early and often to see who actually wants to buy their solution and to define their typical customer. When I meet with startups, I often find that they haven't thought about this enough."

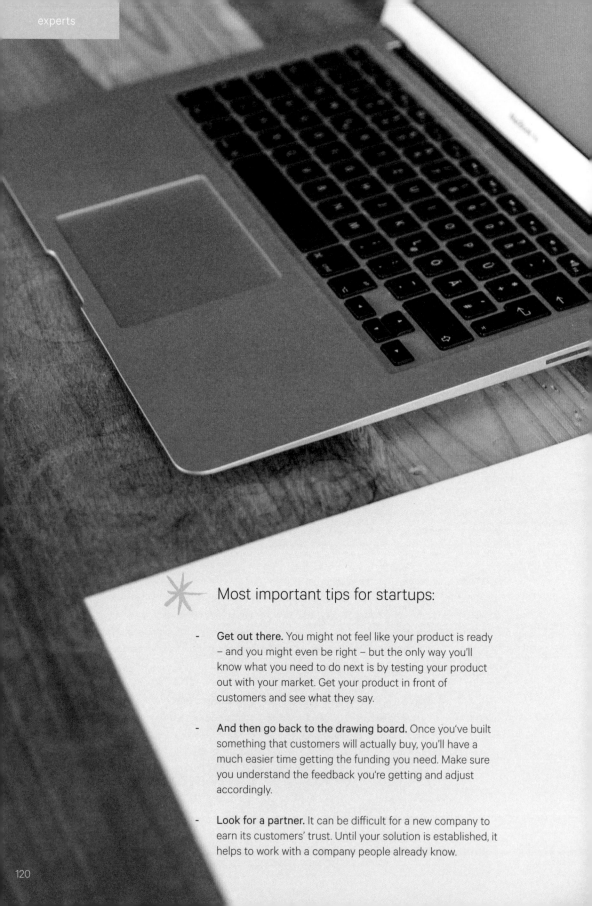

Most important tips for startups:

- **Get out there.** You might not feel like your product is ready – and you might even be right – but the only way you'll know what you need to do next is by testing your product out with your market. Get your product in front of customers and see what they say.

- **And then go back to the drawing board.** Once you've built something that customers will actually buy, you'll have a much easier time getting the funding you need. Make sure you understand the feedback you're getting and adjust accordingly.

- **Look for a partner.** It can be difficult for a new company to earn its customers' trust. Until your solution is established, it helps to work with a company people already know.

Access to test customers is one of the key areas where Raiffeisen Switzerland can help. The bank is actively working to develop Switzerland's fintech ecosystem and offers startups support in a variety of areas. If the bank decides to partner with your company, it can get your product in front of its 3.7 million customers nationwide, giving you a much bigger test audience. It can also help you to figure out what that test audience is thinking: the bank can conduct customer surveys for you, and then help you analyze the data you get back so you can see who's buying your product and why. Once you know exactly what it is your customers want, and once you've had a chance to refine your product, the bank can help you find ways to scale. "We can help you do faster market testing. We have our own test markets, and we can help you create a pilot project."

The bank itself doesn't offer traditional seed capital yet, but it works with startups to implement specific projects. These projects can offer startups essential proofs of concept, which can mean a lot when they do look for funding: a startup can go to investors with the seal of approval of the country's third largest bank.

"We see our role as developing and cocreating the products of interesting startups and helping them implement them," says Patrick. "And when a startup has a big bank as one of its first customers, its value really increases substantially."

About

Raiffeisen is the third largest banking group in Switzerland and a leader in retail banking. Its unique strength lies in its local connections and mindset, which have shaped its business over the past hundred years. 3.7 million Swiss citizens trust it for its business competence, its innovation-oriented products and its fair business practices.

"We see our role as developing and cocreating the products of interesting startups and helping them implement them."

Bernd Brandl and Maria Luisa Silva / SAP Startup Focus

Managing Director, SAP Switzerland / Global Director of Market Enablement and GTM, SAP Startup Focus

The SAP Startup Focus program was launched in 2012 with the mission to help promising startups target the enterprise customer market with solutions in big data, predictive and real-time analytics, artificial intelligence, machine learning, augmented and virtual reality, IoT, and blockchain. The aim is to develop new applications on top of SAP's transformational technology (SAP HANA and SAP Leonardo on the SAP Cloud Platform), and to help accelerate startups' market traction. In May 2013, Prof. Dr. h.c. Hasso Plattner, the chairman of the SAP supervisory board, said, "This is one of the best ideas in the last ten years. This is the future of SAP." Five years after its inception, the program has engaged over six thousand startups operating in twenty-five industries across fifty-eight countries.

The first step for a startup entering the program is to submit its solution online, explaining how SAP technology fits into its strategy. Because Startup Focus is an invitation-only program, the startup will have to wait for feedback on its application. If successful, it'll kick-start with the development acceleration phase, which consists of developing its solution with the support of SAP solution architects and technical experts. Once this phase is accomplished, the startup graduates to the go-to-market phase, where it gains access to SAP's global customer base to showcase and sell its validated solutions. To this day, over three hundred startups have developed commercially viable products that leverage the advantages of the corporation's groundbreaking technology.

"We're building an ecosystem of open innovation based on the creation of value-driven technology solutions by our startup partners," says Maria Luisa Silva, global director of market enablement and GTM at SAP Startup Focus. "Together we address our customers' challenges and accelerate the journey towards digital transformation." SAP's mission of innovating spreads throughout various channels in Switzerland. As a mentor, SAP Switzerland's Co-Innovation Lab (COIL) is a well-distributed network across thirteen geographically dispersed facilities, with the purpose of harnessing SAP's existing ecosystem and successfully enabling high-value, co-innovated business solutions. As a channel for startups, SAP provides opportunities for direct customer engagements with startups that have developed their solutions using SAP technology. Noteworthy engagements have been executed with clients mainly in financial services but also in the utilities, travel and leisure industries. As a networking platform, SAP provides startups with opportunities to present their innovations to interested audiences.

Most important tips for startups:

- **Validate your solution with your target industry:**
  Be aware of your target markets and how to enter
  them before actually trying to do so.

- **The market operates at hyperspeed, so you should
  keep ahead of the game:** Partner with strong technology
  partners that will support and accelerate your market
  traction.

- **Build pilots and leverage these as credibility stamps:**
  Find a reliable base technology that can accelerate your
  growth and represent a strategic partnership towards
  success.

A company SAP was involved with is DayOne. It's a networking platform that was initiated by BaselArea.swiss, a local agency promoting the city of Basel as a center for innovation and business. DayOne serves as an innovation hub for precision medicine, aiming to bring inspiration, collaboration and exposure to various stakeholders. SAP engages actively in this community, contributing to its life science insights and helping the participants – who range from corporates and academics to startups – to advance their innovation initiatives and successfully bring their ideas to market.

Bern-based startup enersis suisse validated from the Startup Focus program in 2016. enersis suisse provides strategic solutions to support its customers' energy transformation. Using the most modern big-data, business-intelligence and visualization technologies, it has developed the software platform GRIDS, which offers various application modules for digital energy services. The program helped enersis suisse as an SAP HANA partner to build its platform and deliver its solution to the market.

Christina Würthner, CFSO at enersis suisse, says, "SAP Startups Focus represents a strategic partnership for us. Currently, we work closely on joint go-to-market routes, for instance by attending notable industry trade fairs and SAP events, such as the Smart City Expo World Congress in Barcelona or the International SAP Conference for Utilities in Lisbon.
We continuously leverage the technical support Startup Focus offers us. Our mission is also to win projects through the SAP Field organization." Through its past IT/SAP consulting activities, enersis suisse has built a closer relationship with SAP in Switzerland, which has lead them to become the first OEM partner in the utilities industry.

"SAP Switzerland has a long-standing history of engaging with the local startup ecosystem," says Bernd Brandl, MD at SAP Switzerland. "We're convinced that innovation and creativity rely on the open exchange of ideas. Innovation is a core value in SAP's vision to help the world run better and improve people's lives, and startups are crucial in its endeavor to help its customers reimagine their businesses because entrepreneurs bring in different attitudes towards solving problems or envisioning new value propositions. It's the power of SAP's technology that eventually makes these innovations possible."

About

SAP founded the Startup Focus Acceleration program in 2012 to build an ecosystem of open innovation. The program shares targeted technology, guidance, and market support, giving entrepreneurs access to the most advanced technology and value-driven offerings to help them deliver innovation at an enterprise scale.

[Contact]   Email: **luisa.silva@sap.com**

[Links]   Web: **startups.sap.com** Twitter: **@SAPStartups**

" We're convinced that innovation and creativity rely on the open exchange of ideas. "

Adrian W. Müller and Jacques Hefti / STARTUP CAMPUS

Head of Center for Innovation and Entrepreneurship / Codirector

Adrian W. Müller and Jacques Hefti have plenty of experience in the startup sector. Adrian founded several lifestyle and luxury businesses and worked as a coach and trainer to help other young companies get off the ground. Jacques, meanwhile, has been working in industry for thirty years. During this time, he cofounded several software and tech companies and still serves on the boards of two of them. He's provided training and support to more than two thousand startups in the Zürich area. With STARTUP CAMPUS, a startup ecosystem and training platform backed by the main universities, techparks and incubators of the region of Zürich, Adrian and Jacques make sure that new companies have the help they need to get going.

"In my opinion, one of the crucial factors for success is a startup's ability to network," says Adrian. He'd know; as the head of the Runway startup incubator, he works to give new businesses the push they need to get started. "It's crucial that you have access to the right startup ecosystem, including investors, trainers and coaches. That's what helps you avoid common pitfalls and minimize the time you need to get your business up and running."

When you're first setting up your business, you'll quickly find that you need more help than you realized. And that doesn't mean just funding; you might also need regulatory and legal advice, insight into your market, staffing support, or help writing a business plan. Jacques, the codirector of STARTUP CAMPUS, says, "The main challenge is not one problem. The main challenge is that you have tons of problems. But as an entrepreneur, you have to focus on what's really important, and that's tough to do when you're young and sometimes a bit naive."

Becoming a part of your local startup ecosystem can help you stay on top of all the challenges you'll face. You'll have the chance to talk to people who have been in your position before, and you'll know what worked for them and what didn't. And if you become an active part, you'll have something even more valuable: a group of potential peers and customers you can test your product and strategies on.

Most important tips for startups:

- **Become part of your ecosystem:** Whatever problem you're facing, someone else has faced it before. If you're plugged into your local entrepreneurial community, you'll see what's worked and what hasn't, and you'll avoid wasting time – and money – reinventing the wheel.

- **Relationships go two ways:** Remember, once you've found an ecosystem or incubator that fits your business, you'll be expected to give as much as you get. But this can be a blessing in disguise: having to produce something your community is interested in means you'll get to do more market testing, with a captive audience.

- **Be a teacher's pet:** If your ecosystem connects you with trainers, remember that they can offer you more than just insight. If they've already succeeded in the local startup environment, they might be able to connect you with the people you'll need to know.

STARTUP CAMPUS provides startups with that ecosystem. When you get started, you'll first go through an extensive training, and following that you get advice on what exactly you need. A company just getting started will need different kinds of help than a company that's ready to start growing. "At the beginning, they need very basic training," says Jacques. "How to make a great pitch, for example. Later they'll need targeted coaching: how to use their IP, for example, or how to build a powerful brand."

New companies don't just pick up new skills; they build their networks. "Those trainings aren't just about learning," Adrian says. "They're about getting in contact with people who have decades of experience and who build connections. Those are the systemic effects that occur when you're part of a whole ecosystem. They're not obvious, but they're absolutely crucial."

One of the startups that STARTUP CAMPUS has worked with, a company called Kinastic, came with a tech idea the founders had developed in the course of their studies: a product that would track your activity when you're at the gym. While Kinastic initially thought their end customers would be individual gym users, they later discovered, with the support and training of STARTUP CAMPUS and particularly the Runway accelerator, their real market was gym operators and health insurance companies. "They came with an idea," says Jacques. "We analyzed their situation, they went through various trainings, and then we could connect them with potential investors. Now they're growing."

About

STARTUP CAMPUS is a platform that connects knowledge and technology transfer, business incubation and the startup ecosystem at the interface of innovation and entrepreneurship. Over the past years it has trained nearly two thousand entrepreneurs whose survival rate after three years is more than 50 percent. STARTUP Campus is backed by the leading universities and tech parks in the greater Zürich area.

[Contact]   Email: **info@startup-campus.ch**

[Links]   Web: **startup-campus.ch** Facebook: **startupcampusost** Twitter: **@StartupCampusCH**

"*The main challenge is not one problem. The main challenge is that you have tons of problems.*"

Andreas Schlenker
/ Tamedia

Head of M&A and Investments at Tamedia within the Classifieds, Marketplaces and Ventures Department

Andreas Schlenker started working with startups in the late 1990s when he left a consulting job in San Francisco to help an internet startup, AllAdvantage.com, scale its European operations. He's been working with startups and venture capital ever since and has spent the past three years investing in digital companies and helping them grow as the head of Tamedia's M&A and Investments activity.

Getting off the ground might seem tough, but growing can be even tougher. "The basic challenge when a company is ready to scale, whether it's B2C or B2B, is having the right product for the right market," says Andreas. "What does that mean? First, addressing the right customer or market need, meaning being able to identify what a target customer or audience really needs. Second, building the product or service accordingly, using the best technology, tools and web services available. The biggest challenge is to marry the two – customer/market needs and product – in an efficient way."

The first thing Andreas would tell you about building your technology or product is that you should see what services and technologies are already commercially available and what you can leverage. For example, Amazon Web Services (AWS) and other cloud services eliminate most companies' needs as far as proprietary server infrastructure and hosting services are concerned.

The second thing can be trickier: when you're trying to scale your company, it will be more important than ever to have the right team around you. "Hiring the right people is key to developing the right product, running an efficient online marketing program and scaling the sales team. It might be the most important step for a startup."

When you're growing, it's essential you have a good CTO and CPO. They'll be the ones working to make sure your product or technology is exactly what it needs to be. You'll also need a good marketing team to make sure you not only really understand your customer but also that you have the right tools to acquire them. Part of building this team is doing the same networking you should be doing anyway: check your own network, go to trade events and leverage social media.

Most important tips for startups:

- **Hire the right people:** You'll be building your product with the team you have, so if the team isn't right, the product won't be either. Make sure you've found a CTO and CPO who are focused on the right things, and that you've assembled the staff they'll need for support.

- **Don't build what you don't need:** Funding and time will be hard to come by when you're still refining your product and learning your market. Don't waste or compromise either one by building anything unnecessary. If there's already a good solution to one of your problems, especially for free, use it.

- **Get the word out:** No matter how great your product is, you'll need a great marketing or sales team to get it in customers' hands, whether that means reaching out to individual B2B clients or figuring out how to best acquire private customers and users.

Helping companies grow is Tamedia's specialty. It invests in startups and successful digital companies for the long term, so it's just as committed to your success as you are. "We try to help our companies recruit the right people. Since we have the experience of having invested in a lot of companies, we can also give good strategic advice or guide you in the right direction on various operational challenges."

Tamedia offers a suite of shared services to all the companies it's invested in. Its tech team, Tamedia Core Engineering and Data Analytics, can help your company build and improve its tech platform as well as better understand your users and usage behavior. Its Online Marketing team helps you develop the right online marketing strategy, the Product Innovation team helps you with product design and UX topics, and the Dealflow team helps bigger portfolio companies find, approach and analyze potential investment and acquisition targets in order to add new services, products and technologies efficiently.

One of Tamedia's best-known Swiss investments might be Doodle, the global online scheduling assistant. Tamedia invested in the company in 2011 as part of an early stage funding round and then acquired the company fully in 2014. At the time of its acquisition, the company had already built a good product and scaled to over twenty-six million monthly users all over the world and was very profitable. Tamedia realized, however, that the company needed to invest even more in technology and its product, and had to adapt its business model, which until then was mainly focused on online advertising. From 2015 on, Tamedia has helped the company triple its staff, further improve its product and initiate a pivot to premium and corporate accounts, a large untapped market. Tamedia achieved all this through close and active interactions with the team, and by enlisting the help of external experts and advisers.

About

Tamedia is the leading private media group in Switzerland. The digital platforms, daily and weekly newspapers and magazines of Tamedia offer general news, dedicated special offerings and classifieds. The company was founded in 1893 and employs a staff of approximately 3,400 in Switzerland, Austria, Denmark, France, Germany, Israel, Luxembourg and Serbia. It has been traded on the Swiss stock exchange since 2000.

[Links]   Web: **tamedia.ch/startup** Twitter: **@Tamedia**

" Hiring the right people is key to developing the right product and scaling a company. It might be the most important step for a startup. "

foun

ders

Melanie Kovacs

Cofounder / Master21

Lots of entrepreneurs create companies to fill gaps they've experienced themselves. Melanie Kovacs is a perfect example: when she couldn't find enough female entrepreneurs to fill a startup weekend, she started the Aspire association to foster diversity in the tech and entrepreneurial space. And after becoming frustrated with the classes she'd taken, she founded her current company, Master21, to make programming education more hands-on.

How did you initially get involved in the entrepreneurial community?
I was interested in entrepreneurship from university on. I participated in a Startup Weekend with a business idea, and afterwards my friend asked me, "Hey, should we pursue this business idea after graduation instead of applying for jobs?" I was skeptical at first, but then I thought, "Why not?" I saw it as a learning opportunity.

So right after the startup weekend in 2013, we started our first company. We didn't register it as a company; it was just a project we worked on in an accelerator. Then I got into organizing startup weekends, and I noticed there was a lack of women taking the stage in Switzerland. There were women participating as attendees but not many who were confidently pitching their ideas. We didn't know a lot of female entrepreneurs we could invite as mentors or judges. That's why I cofounded the Aspire association to foster female entrepreneurship. We did an exhibition where we portrayed twenty-seven female entrepreneurs in Switzerland, and afterwards we did a mentoring program for aspiring female entrepreneurs where we connected them with established entrepreneurs as mentors.

But after that, you spent some time working for an established company. What prompted the change?

After doing many different passion projects that didn't pay my rent, I wanted to have a full-time job in a cool company, so it came in handy that one of the entrepreneurs we interviewed offered me a job in a digital agency called Ginetta. Ginetta is self-managed and offers a lot of chances to work entrepreneurially.

That's how I got into the digital agency business, and then one activity just led to the other. I never planned to work in a digital agency, but I'm glad I received this opportunity. That's where the idea for Master21 was born. All of a sudden, I was around developers, but I had a business background so I had no idea about computers and coding and so forth, and I wanted to learn more. So I signed up for a part-time course at university. The class was super theoretical and instructor-led, just eight hours of typing whatever the instructor was teaching, and the professor had spent all his life in academia. It was not the best learning experience.

I thought it was a really important subject and I was really motivated in the beginning, but in the end, all my colleagues were saying, "Computer science, programming, that's not for me; I'm too stupid," because they couldn't get into it that way or they thought it wasn't fun.

I don't think everybody needs to become a programmer nowadays, but it helps to have a certain understanding of computational thinking. That's how the idea of Master21 was born. We wanted to teach these critical twenty-first-century skills in a more hands-on way with teachers who were actually working in the industry and who had relevant experience.

You've done a lot of work to promote diversity in tech. Why do you think there's not enough diversity in tech?

It's a tough question. There are two different aspects. One aspect is that women in tech and female entrepreneurs in general are missing role models. What you can't see, you can't be. It's a famous saying, but I think it's true. At around age four, kids start to correlate careers with gender. And if they don't see women entrepreneurs or programmers, they think they don't belong.

Once girls and women are attracted to tech, the "how to learn" aspect is important. In terms of learning, there aren't a lot of options in Switzerland at the moment. Either you study computer science at university, which takes three years, or you do an apprenticeship.

"Nowadays you can do anything but not everything at once, so you have to decide where you want to go and really focus on that."

But with both options, you don't program a lot. It's primarily the theoretical computer science part. People don't really learn programming languages. Most people learn to program by themselves. You can do an online course, but as a lot of studies show, there's a high dropout rate. So there are not many options for how to learn: it's either at a university, which is super theoretical; or online, which requires a lot of patience and discipline.

Everyone who wants to do a programming boot camp at Master21 tells me that they've tried to learn programming online and it didn't work for them. It's the same as doing sports: if you get a gym membership, you pay and commit and get to know the people and have a regular schedule. It's social and there's a structure, so it's easier to keep up. With an online course, you're by yourself, and if you encounter a problem you can find the answer online but it might take forever.

How did Master21 grow after you founded it?

I started it in 2016 when I was still employed at Ginetta. I kept talking about this idea in my head until my boyfriend gave me a kick in the ass. He said, "Let's build a website and take it live and see if people are actually interested." I guess I was kind of annoying him! So we took the website live in August 2016 and did the first boot camp in October. We offered two different programs and did pilots of both. We wanted to put one course out there, get the feedback, improve it, and go from there. And that's pretty much what we did for all of 2017. For all the courses we offer, we improved along the way all the time. We'll keep doing it that way. It's essential to keep getting feedback from attendees and to continuously improve.

What's been the hardest part so far?

Really just starting. That was the hardest part. The other hard part is that there are endless possibilities. Nowadays you can do anything but you can't do everything at once, so you have to decide where you want to go and really focus on that. You have to be clear on what you want to do, and that's not always so easy. A lot of people approach you, and you have this opportunity and that partnership, but you have only limited time and energy. Focusing is always a struggle.

Have you seen diversity improving?

Yeah, it's great. In our courses, about 70 percent of our students so far have been women, even though we only did one program so far that was exclusively for women. In the beginning, we didn't intentionally focus on that; we just kind of attracted a lot of women. I don't know why. It could be because I'm the head of it and I'm well connected in these networks. It could also be just because it's a time when a lot of women want to do something and are ambitious – they want to learn and grow.

What advice would you give to people getting into tech or founding their own companies?
Just start. For me at least, if you overthink it too much, you see more and more obstacles, and people will try to talk you out of it. The goal seems higher and higher and harder and harder to reach. But if you start, you get these little "yay" moments – these small successes – and you build confidence along the way. You can grow and continue that way. It's impossible to foresee everything at the beginning, but once you're on the way, you see lots of opportunities that you didn't see before.

But maybe start small. For example, I hear a lot of people say, "I want to open a restaurant," and I think, "Why not have a pop-up shop or a food stand or something to experiment with first and see if you like it?" In the end, you'll invest a lot of time into this, so you need to like this kind of business. It should suit your strengths and interests. Start small and experiment. That's what I did with the first company I started right after business school, and with the Aspire association. I didn't know what to do after business school, so I worked on different projects, and as a result I got to know a lot of people and learned a lot. In the end, I decided I wanted to work in a small company and do something with communication and working with clients. The job offer in the agency suited me really well.

How is Zürich as a place to found a company?
It's a great place. I see a lot of potential in Zürich. It's always a bit slower than other cities, but there are a lot of people with potential, a lot of ideas. And I love working at Impact Hub; it's an important part of the ecosystem. It's a great community and it has supported us from the start.

[About]   Master21 wants people to thrive in the twenty-first century. To achieve this, Master21 creates transformative learning experiences where people learn skills like coding, critical thinking and creativity.

[Links]   Web: **master21.academy** Facebook: **master21academy** Twitter: **master21academy**

What are your top work essentials?
A quiet space, a Kanban board, and lots of Post-its.
And obviously my MacBook.

At what age did you found your company?
I founded Aspire at twenty-five, and Master21 at
twenty-eight.

What's your most used app?
Things and Basecamp

**What's the most valuable piece of advice you've been
given?**
None – I prefer to think for myself.

What's your greatest skill?
Connecting the dots – connecting people and topics.

151

David Allemann

Cofounder / On

David Allemann, Caspar Coppetti, and three-time World Duathlon champion and multiple Ironman winner Olivier Bernhard started On in 2010 to produce radical new running shoes that would give runners "the perfect running sensation." Seven years later, On shoes are available at over three thousand retailers in more than fifty countries and counting.

What motivated you to start a shoe company?

Three of us founded the company, but Olivier was the one who came to Caspar and me with an idea that he'd stumbled upon. It was still very much a prototype, but he said, "Hey, give this a try." At first, we told him he was completely insane – no one starts a running shoe company against the big guys, and out of Switzerland of all places. But he said, "Just step into the shoe." When we did, we had the same reaction that three million runners have now had: "Wow, that feels different." And that convinced us to form a team and a company around that unique running sensation. If the shoe hadn't been convincing on its own, we would have basically had to just outmarket the bigger guys, and that's not possible; but since we truly had a product that feels different and looks different, we thought we had a fighting chance.

It's fantastic to look back now seven years later and see that On has become the fastest grow-ing running shoe company on the planet. We're the fastest brand in terms of adding new fans.

What's your background?

I have a little bit of an eclectic background. A lawyer by training, I cofounded one of the first digital agencies in Switzerland, joined McKinsey as a management consultant, then led the advertising agency Y&R. Before On, I was CMO of Vitra, one of the most interesting design and furniture brands. I've always been in this space where business meets creativity and ideas.

How did you meet your cofounders?

Caspar and I had worked at McKinsey and Y&R together, which means we've had a long and very productive working relationship for almost fifteen years. And Caspar was Olivier's athletic manager during his studies. We've been fortunate to form true friendships across our team.

How was the process of starting the company? How did you take this from a prototype to a new company?

Small and fast. We started in our living rooms and applied for the brand new ISPO award. ISPO is the largest sports fair in Europe and across the globe. They do a newcomer award, so we sent them our prototype. A few weeks later, they called us and told us we'd won the overall award. They said it was an amazing shoe, they'd tested it out, and they were all big fans. So when we came to ISPO, all the billboards were plastered with big pictures of our shoes. We had retailers and distributors left and right telling us, "Wow, we'd love to sell your shoe, but we need it by June so the season isn't over." This was in February. We knew we had to have a final shoe within five months. So I got on a plane to spend the next three months in Asia to ensure that we had the perfect shoe.

How does a small, new company compete in an established market like running shoes?

I think what's interesting over the last fifteen years is that product became more important again and marketing dollars became less important. Through digital channels, you can know exactly what others say about the product. Our biggest marketing tool is actually putting someone in the shoe and giving them a better product, a better running sensation, a better experience. People are enthusiastic to share that.

How did you begin growing your audience?

We went to lots of events. We are doing more than three, four hundred events per year with the simple goal to get people into On shoes and share the sensation you have when you step into an On. At the same time, we have fantastic allies. Three thousand of the best running shoe specialist retailers have joined our fan group, and they're putting thousands of runners into On shoes every day.

What's been the hardest part or the biggest challenge?

We've been very committed from the very beginning that we only want to work with the best people. We said, "Hey, if we want to build not only a product but a lasting organization that keeps innovating beyond our current dreams, then we have to find the very best people and form a fantastic team." And finding the best people fast enough has been the hardest challenge.

" It's not like we had quiet lives in the past and now we're boarding a rocket ship. The difference is that now we can fly the rocket ship ourselves and decide on the star we want to reach. "

How do you mean?

We have very high expectations. We don't hire for skills but for personality and the ability to constantly learn and grow as a person. Finding people who are exceptionally gifted and great to work with is simply hard. Out of one hundred applications, we hire one person. If you're growing as fast as On does, basically doubling the size of the company every year, then that's a big challenge. And we don't want to compromise, obviously.

How does a new company start setting up international supply chains?

We're not coming from the running shoe business, so we had never built a running shoe. That's at first a disadvantage because you don't know any of the players and manufacturers. At the same time, it's an advantage because you're questioning everything and finding new routes to success. So when we went out, we first had to find the right manufacturers, and that's not just one partner but a whole ecosystem of partners: the best mold-maker, the best producer of highly technical mesh, the best factory that can do complicated injection soles, and at the end some very passionate craftsmen and -women to assemble the perfect shoe.

How has your own life changed since founding a company?

It's a wild adventure. You can grow something, and it very fundamentally enhances people's running experience. It's fantastic to see how people are coming back with a smile after their first run in an On shoe. Seeing that across the globe, especially in very unexpected places, is very gratifying.

At the same time, if you've done several very different things in life that range from design to tech to advertising and sports, building your own company feels like everything is coming together and falling into place. It's not just one specialized function that you're doing; you have to be super versatile and do something completely different in the afternoon from what you did in the morning, and you're probably going to do something next year that's completely different from what you did the year before.

Is there anything you don't like about the founder's lifestyle?

Yes, but in a positive way. I do lots more sports. It's the very fabric of the company, so it's not just that I can do sports in the evening or over the weekend; at On, at almost every point in time during the day, someone is doing sports.

My personal life hasn't really changed that much since founding On. I think that's our experience as founders: we've always been really passionate about what we're doing. If you're passionate about something, you obviously do it a lot. It's not like we had quiet lives in the past and now we're boarding a rocket ship. The difference is that now we can fly the rocket ship ourselves and decide on the star we want to reach.

What kind of advice would you give to new founders?

Probably two things. First, do it together with the best people. Second, if you know in your gut that something isn't right or that you have to change something, make it happen and act immediately. In nine out of ten cases, that's the right decision to make rather than to wait to make sure it isn't the one out of ten. If you do that, you lose valuable time. That's a little bit of the culture at On too. If you're not sure if you should do something, you do it.

Can you give me an example?

We weren't sure, for example, whether we should do a new type of sole made out of this new much lighter foam. That was just two years into the life of the company, and we had this completely new sole in our hands because On is constantly innovating. We weren't sure if it was too early. We didn't know if we should come out with the next big thing so soon, or first let the market digest what we'd just launched.

We decided you can't be too fast when it comes to innovation. And this shoe with the sole made of Zero-Gravity foam is our absolute best seller today.

How is Zürich as a place to found a company?

It's a very special place. First of all, Zürich has been awarded the best place for quality of life on the planet multiple times. You're out in nature immediately, you have a lake, you have mountains. It's obviously the perfect playground for a sports company.

It's also a great place to attract people; people love to come to Zürich. And it's a place where you have many nationalities. We're a young and global company that operates in fifty different markets, so we have more than forty nationalities. So being in a very international city that still kind of has a manageable size and a great quality of life is a great place to start a young company.

[About] On is the fastest-growing running community on the planet. With offices in Zürich (Switzerland), Portland (Oregon, USA), Yokohama (Japan), Melbourne (Australia) and São Paulo (Brazil), the young Swiss sports company has become a global innovator in the running shoe and apparel space. On has one simple mission: make running fun. A team of sports scientists, world-class athletes and designers spearhead this mantra.

[Links]   Web: on-running.com Facebook: onrunning Twitter: @on_running Instagram: on_running

What are your top work essentials?
A clean desk.

At what age did you found your company?
Forty.

What's your most used app?
These days, probably Slack.

What's the most valuable piece of advice you've been given?
Read a lot.

What's your greatest skill?
Creating an image of how something should be and then bringing it to reality.

Christian Kaufmann

Cofounder, Head of Operations and Finance / WeAct

Christian Kaufmann grew up around the world, living in the United Arab Emirates, Honduras, Spain, the USA, Greece and Chile, in addition to his native Switzerland. He finished his master's degree in management in Lausanne before cofounding WeAct, a platform designed to help companies create fun and engaging sustainability and health programs.

You've lived in quite a few places. Why did your family travel so much?
It was mainly because of my father's work. He's a project manager at a company called Rheinmetall, which is a defense contractor. Whenever the company has a project with a foreign government, they normally have a knowledge transfer; my father is the liaison between both entities. We'd go to the host country for the duration of the project, normally three to five years, return to Switzerland in between, and then move again.

After being born in Switzerland, I spent the first four years in Abu Dhabi. My kindergarten time I spent in a small town in Switzerland called Aarburg, then I went back to Abu Dhabi to finish primary school. Then we went for one year to Honduras, where my mother is actually from. I finished high school in San Sebastian, in Basque Country in Spain, and did my studies in the USA, Greece, Switzerland and Chile.

What kind of work did you do before you started working with WeAct?
After I finished my bachelor's degree in Greece in business administration, I spent six months working for Apple computers, in an IT support call center. That was one of my first professional experiences. It wasn't that interesting, but I learned a lot about Apple products, which I was quite passionate about at the time.

Then I returned to Zürich and got an opportunity to work for Credit Suisse in Zürich as a junior client manager in the Employee Stock Options Services. It was my second big experience in the corporate world, and I realized it wasn't right for me: it was very hierarchical,

very structured, more based on a numbers-only approach. I worked there for nine months, and I didn't enjoy it very much. I felt that it was very restrictive. Everyone had a suit and tie on every day, and it just didn't feel like the kind of environment I wanted to work in. It actually made me not want to work in a traditional company at all. There was this formal and constrictive culture, which was very uninspiring. There are thousands of employees working in so many divisions and departments, each one in their own little bubble where you have a limited view of the global picture and even less sense of truly contributing to making a difference.

So I started thinking about careers that were more in line with my values and my way of working, so to speak. I did a few other jobs after that, mainly in consulting, but in all my work experience, this profit-driven mindset didn't really appeal to me, nor did the traditional hierarchy structure. I'd always had a problem following orders just for the sake of following orders.

Was there a sort of last straw?
It was a combination of things. After working for two years, I realized a business degree from Greece was preventing me from advancing in the business world, so I decided to do a master's degree at the University of Lausanne. During that time, I took a social entre-preneurship class, which was one of the best classes I've ever taken. The class had a theoretical part that taught us about this new business approach to solving societal and environmental problems, but at the same time it had a practical part that was set up as a team competition among the participating students to help a future social startup, jobfactory, develop various areas of its business, with the winner getting a $10,000 prize to implement the project.

My team and I won the competition, and for the first time I was really captivated by the idea of working for something that was not just profit-driven but also trying to create a sustainable solution to a problem in society. It was an eye-opener for me to see how companies don't have to all be corporate-driven – that they can also solve problems with more flexible, innovative structures.

How did you have the idea for WeAct? How'd the company get started?
I joined WeAct in 2012, but the idea actually started in 2010 with two people, Majka Baur and Prisca Müller, the two other cofounders who attended the Ecoworkshop at ETH, the technical university of Zürich, where the main goal was to find innovative ideas to reduce CO_2 emissions on campus. Instead of thinking of new technology that would solve the problem, they focused on how to motivate people to use the existing solutions. They wanted to find ways to get people to undertake daily actions that have a positive environmental impact, and so the WeAct Challenge was born.
They won this competition and received some money with which they created the first

" *The entrepreneurship world is all about moving forward. You're building the future, and you're responsible for that future.* "

WeAct Association, and they started implementing their idea with the students on campus. They did this for two years – 2010 and 2011 – and after graduating in 2012, they decided to transition it from a student project into a social startup. They began defining the business model around it and started looking for a person with a business background who could help them with the value proposition and customer acquisition. This was at the end of my master's program in the fall of 2012. We got to know each other, and I started working with them on a trial basis for a month without getting paid. We clicked so well that I became part of the team. Then, a year and a half later in March 2014, we decided to incorporate and switch from an association to an LLC.

How has this been different from the corporate world?
One of the negative things about working at a social startup is that there's normally not that much funding. That means you have to get by with a much lower income, at least much lower than you'd be paid in the corporate world. But that also leads to one of the positives: the people who work here are very, very purpose-driven. Everyone who works at a social startup is really committed to the purpose you're trying to achieve. In our case, it's about creating a society that's more in harmony with the environment, where everyone has the ecological footprint of one person rather than three people.

With such a committed team, you don't have to have the same kind of structures of control and accountability because you know that everyone's here because they want to be. You can give everyone more freedom because you're all working towards the same goal.

The other thing is that the entrepreneurship world is all about moving forward. You're building the future, and you're responsible for that future. In the corporate world I was just another number. I didn't feel like I could influence the big picture.

Is it easier for smaller startups than for larger companies to address social problems?
Yes, I'd definitely say it is. Startups in general are very explorative and need to adapt to new environmental and market conditions. The innovation aspect can be quite limited within a corporation due to their internal processes, especially if that corporation is publicly traded, because it will be very result-driven and there will be a lot of pressure from shareholders.

The other obstacle for a large company is financial myopia. When you present anything to the CEO or CFO in a big company, it has to either improve revenue or decrease costs. It's all in financial terms. Other impact criteria seem irrelevant to them. If you can't monetize something, the chances of it being dismissed are much higher.

But the two worlds aren't actually so far apart. The reality is that most of the social startups I know of are dependent on big corporations as a source of revenue, either in the form of clients or sponsors. Corporate responsibility is a topic that's been growing, and there are more social startups that can cater to corporations' responsibility needs. In our case, our mission is to change the habits of people to encourage a more sustainable lifestyle and create a healthier corporate culture. We're looking for ways to engage employees on the topic of sustainability so they can think about it in their work. So there's a certain symbiosis between those two sides – corporations fund social startups like ours to improve their own culture. Big corporations can be too stagnant or too slow to try new things, so they rely on social startups to take the first step.

How do you like Zürich as a place to run a business?
On the one hand, it's an incredible place because it offers a really high quality of life. You have a really clean, diverse city, and the nature is really close. In half an hour, you're on a mountain or in a forest.

The negative side is that Swiss culture is sometimes too organized. Having grown up in different places, chaotic places, you get used to a bit more freedom and flexibility, and you also have more warmness, which you kind of lack in Zürich. But Zürich is a great place to found a social startup. There are many foundations and institutions to support companies that try to make a positive social or environmental impact, and you're actually quite likely to get some seed money to get it started.

[About]   **WeAct is an ETH spin-off that develops innovative and interactive engagement programs (WeAct Challenges) to promote sustainability, health and cooperation within organizations. The Challenges are real-life and team-based competitions that use the power of gamification and team dynamics in an online platform to provide participants with a learning-by-doing experience of what it means to live a sustainable lifestyle.**

[Links]   Web: weact.ch Facebook: weact.ch Twitter: @weACT_ch Instagram: weactchallenge

What are your top work essentials?
Definitely my phone and my MacBook.

At what age did you found your company?
Thirty-one.

What's your most used app?
I really love music, so Spotify.

What's the most valuable piece of advice you've been given?
I think to choose my career wisely, meaning not to choose money over purpose.

What's your greatest skill?
Because I was raised in several countries, I developed a lot of empathy and understanding.

Cristina Riesen

Founder and CEO / We Are Play Lab

Cristina Riesen has been founding, working in and mentoring startups for years. After working with Silicon Valley–based Evernote for more than five years, she wanted to do something bigger than creating a new app: she wanted to help reshape how we educate our children, which she describes as one of the biggest problems we're facing today. As a result, she started We Are Play Lab in January 2017.

Could you describe We Are Play Lab's mission?
When you ask yourself, "How can we fix education today?" it seems like a massive undertaking. It's huge – where do you start? The more I looked into the topic, the more I realized that re-engineering twenty-first-century education doesn't have that much to do with technology. There's a lot of focus put on adding layers of technology to education or adapting curricula, but I think it goes well beyond that. It's really about re-engineering mindsets and beliefs and attitudes. We have to ask ourselves what it is we're educating our children for. What is the goal of education? It certainly is not to get a diploma. Today, especially in our fast-paced world, it has more to do with skills that have not been embedded in the formal education system, like curiosity, persistence, creativity and critical thinking.

I think we need to come together from different areas and different disciplines and look at how humans learn best because we don't have to reinvent the wheel; there are best practices that have been out there for thousands of years. Transforming education has to do with first understanding the science of learning and then using technology to help people learn for life in the best possible way. It also has to do with spaces where learning can happen, involving urban planning, architecture and neuroscience. All in all, we have to get out of the box and start to move away from education and instead focus on learning and the purpose of learning, and on how we can empower our children to become creators.

I am optimistic by nature. People say there are so many challenges relating to technology and education, but I think there's tremendous opportunity out there.

How does We Are Play Lab work?

We're a non-profit, for-purpose community, and we're developing initiatives and experiences and products for short-term, medium-term and long-term impacts. We're exploring different ways we can design interventions in public spaces to support parents and educators and communities on the one hand, and then give them tools so they know what to do with these opportunities.

We recently launched the first prototype of Project Parkopolis in Switzerland as part of a global initiative called "Transforming Cities into Learning Landscapes." This initiative is among the big ideas being used to re-imagine cities as extraordinary learning opportunities. Kids spend most of their time awake outside of school, so we're looking at how you can support learning in everyday environments.

The prototype is a life-sized board game based on years of research from the science of learning. It's been done with a world-class researcher team from the science of learning, led by Kathy Hirsch-Pasek, who is also a senior fellow at the Brookings Institution Center for Universal Education. This life-sized board game takes children, and also educators and parents, through this process of learning twenty-first-century skills. Children have to create their own rules for this game. By design, all activities happening in Parkopolis encourage not only computational thinking and digital skills but also critical thinking, creativity and collaboration, so this is a very basic, affordable, almost deceptively simple intervention showing people what is possible and also showing how, if you want your kids to become more creative or to understand how technology works, it's not a question of having them spend hours and hours in front of a computer. This is the very first public intervention that we are working on, and others will follow.

What made you start We Are Play Lab?

As a mother and someone coming from the tech world, I was personally very frustrated with the current state of education. I think that education is not only one of the biggest challenges we have today but also one of the biggest opportunities. It just cannot be that we cannot solve it. It's not about trying to infuse every classroom with thousands of apps and technology; it's about coming together as a society and trying to figure out how we can work together to transform the way we teach our kids – because it's not just educators or policymakers who should be under pressure to change education. It's really all of us: parents, caregivers, entrepreneurs, companies, cities.

"*There are so many people who don't get those opportunities, and it's so much wasted human potential. I think we can change that.*"

We should not underestimate the power of the small steps and contributions we can make on a daily basis. This is why, aside from founding We Are Play Lab, I also helped launch the Swiss Tech Collider, the very first edtech community in Switzerland. It's on the campus of EPFL, the Swiss Federal Institute of Technology in Lausanne, one of the leading technical universities in the world. This year, in the beginning of April, we officially launched this space; now it's more than sixty edtech startups coming together, and I think it's great. There are so many synergies and potential for disruptive innovation among these startups.

What did you do before founding We Are Play Lab?
Well, I like lateral moves in life, so I was doing lots of different things. I was born in Romania, and after I finished studying I worked at a radio station for a few years before moving to Switzerland and continuing my studies in communications and PR. While doing my executive master of science in communications management, I decided to launch my first company. That was in 2010. Back then, nobody knew what to do with social media and digital communications. I felt that it would change the world of communication forever, and I took the plunge and launched my company.

I was actually quite happy with my project, but then a friend of mine tweeted that Evernote was looking for somebody in communications in Europe. I was not necessarily looking for a job, but I was a huge fan of Evernote, so I knew it had to be me. I joined Evernote as the first hire in Europe and stayed with them for five years. I was the general manager for Europe, the Middle East and Africa, and led the communication, marketing and sales team in the region. That was an exciting time, being part of such an amazing global company early on. It was the really intensive early growth phase, growing from 50 people to 250.

But after five years you're a bit of a dinosaur in the startup world, and I felt it was time for me to challenge myself and move on to the next level. I knew that the next big thing was education. I was obsessively asking how we could do something to support kids around the world in fulfilling their potential. What could we do to ensure they have equal access to high-quality education? If I design a fancy app today, it's going to be for just a fortunate few, but what we're looking at is how we can provide world-class, high-quality learning in the twenty-first century for every kid, especially those who are not given the opportunity.

Building We Are Play Lab also has to do with my personal story. I was born in Romania in a modest family under the communist government. Throughout my life, had I not been given the opportunity to study, or the opportunity to try different things and be part of different life-changing projects, I wouldn't be who I am today. Being given that opportunity is extremely important. I see many people who don't get those opportunities, and it's so much wasted human potential. I think we can change that.

What are the different challenges a non-profit startup faces?
Based on my experience so far, it's ten times more difficult to be a nonprofit startup. The biggest challenge is figuring out how we build a new model in a way that has a real impact in the world. It's not easy.

The whole world of nonprofits is actually quite new to me, so I'm learning on the job and simultaneously challenging the model. When looking at the current state of NGOs and the well-established startup model, I'm continuously asking myself if there's a better way we could bring the two together. The more I look into it, the more I see that we need to move away from framing an organization as profit/nonprofit. I think it's simply not going to be possible for companies to ignore the real impact they have in the world. We need to rethink the value chain: the products we're creating, for whom they're intended, the impact of building them, and the impact on the people working on building them, and so on.

What's the biggest challenge so far?
Every day presents itself with a new challenge. It's extreme highs and extreme lows. This is true for any entrepreneur, whether you're nonprofit or for-profit, it doesn't matter. Entrepreneurship isn't for everybody, and it should not be romanticized. We must stop telling people that everyone should be an entrepreneur because honestly they shouldn't; it is really hard.

This is especially true when you have crazy new ideas. People will just laugh at you or simply ignore you because your idea doesn't make sense to them, so you have to brace yourself for a tough ride. Most importantly, you need to learn to build your own personal safe zone and not to take everything personally.

[About]   We Are Play Lab empowers children with the skills, attitudes and knowledge they need to thrive in a fast-paced, increasingly complex world. It elevates the public discourse around the breadth of skills needed in the twenty-first century and supports parents, educators and communities in transforming ordinary places into extraordinary education opportunities through playful learning.

What are your top work essentials?
Coffee, I have to go with that.

At what age did you found your company?
I was thirty-something when I founded my first.

What's your most used app?
I use Evernote for productivity and Headspace for mindfulness.

What's the most valuable piece of advice you've been given?
I read this and it stuck with me: "If they don't give you a seat at the table, bring a folding chair."

What's your greatest skill?
Persistence.

Pascal Mathis and Lukas Weder

Partners / Wingman

Lukas Weder and Pascal Mathis have each been through the entire startup lifecycle, having grown companies from ideas to businesses to exits. With Wingman, a startup advice and consulting firm they founded in 2016, they're bringing their experience to new founders.

How did the two of you get involved in the startup community?
Lukas: We each founded our own startups about ten years ago. I founded EAT.ch, and Pascal founded GetYourGuide. EAT.ch is the biggest food delivery portal in Switzerland. It's like Lieferheld or Lieferando in Germany. We built it over ten years and then sold it to the market leader, Just Eat, in London. And GetYourGuide is the biggest portal for tourist attractions worldwide. Pascal started it in 2008, and now it has over fifteen million monthly active users. The ecosystem in Switzerland is not too big, and we actually met at a startup conference. We kept in contact after that.

How did you come up with the ideas for your first companies?
Pascal: I was just talking with some friends over lunch about how easy is it to book flights and hotels over the internet, and we were asking ourselves why it was so hard to book experiences. We started to think we could change that: we could make a service that would also allow people to book tours and activities.

Lukas: As students, we saw the same business model as EAT.ch working really well in Copenhagen, so we thought, let's try to set up the same thing in Switzerland and see if it works here, too. We tried it out, and it worked. Then in 2011, Just Eat launched a partnership to get access to the Swiss market.

So what does your current company Wingman do?

Lukas: Wingman is a startup-consulting company. We advise startups and help them grow, so it's a founder-to-founder consulting company. We think people who have already done it themselves know some of the most common obstacles founders will have and how they can be solved best. We work with startups in a lot of different fields, in both new and established areas, and advise them on their business plan, fundraising, marketing, whatever. We're kind of a sparring partner for the founders. They run their ideas past us, and we figure out what problems they might have and how to fix them.

We think the name is important. A wingman doesn't help you fly the plane but stays behind you and guards your back. We're not copilots; we're wingmen. We don't tell startups what to do; we just help them get to their destination on their own.

Pascal: We started angel-investing three or four years ago and realized that while money is one part, the other thing that startups need is the know-how, advice and experience. We didn't have time to do this while we had day jobs as investors, so we decided to start Wingman to focus more on that side of it.

When a startup works with Wingman, what's the process like? How do you help them?

Pascal: Since we're business angels, we like getting to know new Swiss startups. Often we're already familiar with a company before we work together. So when a company needs advice or hits some kind of obstacle, they come for coffee and present their ideas and plans, and we see if they have a problem we can help with. This issue might be how to open the next office in a new market, how to deal with a partner or how to fundraise more effectively – something like that.

Lukas: We also offer very different kinds of advice for different fields. Startups often come to us when they first need advice or they're first getting started and ask us to help them with their fundraising process. What we typically do then is we sharpen their business model, we do a nice investor story, we do high-level financials, we define the amount of capital that's required and we advise them on what kind of investor they should reach out to. When a startup's at a different stage of its growth, it might come to us with other problems. These often include how to grow their business, how to do all the hiring stuff and so on. But it's most common that we help during the fundraising process. That can be one of the most difficult stages for a new company, and our connections within the Swiss startup community can really help clients find the right direction to look in.

«At some point in every company's story, it finds out that the market isn't right or the product has to change a little bit. A smart team is able to do this and make changes.»

What makes fundraising in particular so difficult?

Pascal: The startups always think they have everything in place: they have the right team, they have a perfect process, the market is right, etc. But what you often find is that they haven't tested these ideas out enough in reality. Once they release their product to the market, they suddenly find that the market is just not big enough, or the business model they had in mind won't work. They don't really know who their customer is or who should pay what for their solution. And these questions aren't easy to answer; they're different for every company. When these startups talk to potential investors, they need to have a lot of these answers already figured out. Investors understand that a new company might need time to refine its offering, but it should have the basics proven already. So that's one of the most difficult parts in getting funding.

To be better prepared, what other kinds of things should a startup pay attention to?

Pascal: After proving the basic concept, the most important thing is always the team. Investors want to see that the two or three or four of you are the right team to make your business successful, that you have the right match of skills to build out your idea, and that you're smart enough and committed enough to the company's success to be able to pivot when you need to. At some point in every company's story, it finds out that the market isn't right or the product has to change a little bit. A smart team is able to do this and make changes. The not-so-smart team isn't able to change direction and is stuck working on a product there's no demand for. Beyond that, investors want to see really good cofounders who are different from each other. It doesn't help you if you all have the same skills.

Lukas: The second challenge we see a lot is how to tell your story to investors in an easy to understand way – how to explain your product and your business model. You have to focus on some clear aspects of the business and make it accessible to investors so they can understand the big picture of what you're offering.

What are some of the biggest struggles your companies have faced?

Pascal: Hiring was always the most difficult for me. Figuring out who you should hire, what position you should hire next. Should you hire a cutting-edge engineer, or the perfect salesperson for the US market? Which position would add more value?

Lukas: For EAT.ch, as with a lot of platform businesses, the hardest part was always having the supply and demand sides ready at the same time. If you're running a food delivery service, as soon as you have a lot of users, it's easier to get the restaurants. Once you get the restaurants, it's easier to get the users. If you have all the restaurants in Switzerland on your platform, it's very easy to get customers to join your portal. But getting either one at first is the tricky part.

How did you deal with that?

Lukas: That's a good question. We pushed on both sides at once: we hired a sales team to get the restaurants on board, and invested a lot of money in marketing on the user side. So we grew both sides together.

How would you describe the Swiss startup scene today?

Pascal: Ten years ago, when we started GetYourGuide and EAT.ch, it wasn't really one of the career paths that students thought about in Switzerland. That's changed a lot since then. People think about starting new companies and innovating in new areas more. The other good thing about the Swiss ecosystem is the good technical universities in Lausanne or Zürich. One way the Swiss startup community is still weak is selling new technologies and doing it at the right time. The US scene in particular is better at selling. We often produce really nice technical solutions here, but we aren't good at marketing them abroad.

Lukas: What's good in the Swiss startup ecosystem at the moment is that we've already had a first generation of successful founders, and these founders are now able to mentor the new generation of startups and invest there as well. Now that we have experienced people here who have done it all already, it's beginning to pick up steam. The new generation has an even better starting point than the guys ten years ago.

Do you miss running startups yourself?

Pascal: I wasn't planning on becoming a business angel for that exact reason. I'm an entrepreneur, and I like doing different things, not just sitting at the exit.

But that's one of the fun things about being a startup consultant: we can go through that process of innovation with ten different companies at the same time. It's not as intense as if you were the founder of the company, but you're still a crucial player in making the business work. Whenever there's a critical situation, the wingman has to get involved and solve it.

[About]   Wingman was founded in 2016 with the mission to help startups throughout their lifespan, from foundation through growth and fundraising rounds, towards a successful exit. The two founders are entrepreneurs themselves and have cofounded the successful companies EAT. ch and GetYourGuide.

[Links]   Web: **wingman.ch**

What are your top work essentials?
Pascal: Internet.

At what age did you found your company?
Lukas: I was twenty-six, if I remember correctly.
Pascal: Twenty-eight.

What's your most used app?
Pascal: Google Maps.

**What's the most valuable piece of
advice you've been given?**
Lukas: I learned that startup life is not a sprint, it's a marathon. It
took me ten years to make my company successful.

What's your greatest skill?
Pascal: I think I connect well with people. I can understand people
quickly.
Lukas: We are definitely very quick at adapting to a new situation,
a new field, a new business model.

directory

The following selection is only a brief choice of organizations, companies and contacts available in the Zürich region.

Startups

Carbon Delta
Feldeggstraße 4
8008 Zürich
carbon-delta.com

CUTISS AG
Weinbergstraße 35
8092 Zürich
cutiss.swiss

ElectricFeel AG
Feldeggstraße 4
8008 Zürich
electricfeel.com

Farmy AG
Buckhauserstraße 28
8048 Zürich
farmy.ch

ImagineCargo
Hohlstraße 400
8048 Zürich
imaginecargo.com

modum.io AG
Technoparkstraße 1
8005 Zürich
modum.io

Renzo Balboa AG
Am Schanzengraben 15
8002 Zürich
balboamove.ch

TestingTime AG
Bahnhofstraße 3
8001 Zürich
testingtime.com

UrbanFarmers AG
Technoparkstrasse 1
8005 Zürich
urbanfarmers.com

Wildbiene + Partner
Heinrichstraße 267A
8005 Zürich
wildbieneundpartner.ch

Programs

Climate-KIC Accelerator
Limmatstraße 264
8005 Zürich
climate-kic-dach.org

Exit Accelerator
Stampfenbachstraße 32
8006 Zürich
exitaccelerator.com

F10 Incubator & Accelerator
Förrlibuckstraße 10
8005 Zürich
f10.ch

Innosuisse – Swiss Promotion Agency
Einsteinstraße 2
3003 Bern
innosuisse.ch

Kickstart Accelerator
c/o Impact Hub Zürich
Viaduktstraße 93
8005 Zürich
kickstart-accelerator.com

STRIDE
c/o Impact Hub Zürich
Viaduktstraße 93
8005 Zürich
stride-learning.ch

Swisscom Digital Business Unit
Konradstraße 12
8005 Zürich
swisscom.com/startup

Swiss Startup Factory Ltd
Dorfstraße 27
8037 Zürich
swissstartupfactory.com

Spaces

BlueLion Incubator
Sihlquai 125
8005 Zürich
bluelion.ch

Büro Züri
Bahnhofstraße 9
8001 Zürich
buero-zueri.ch

daycrunch
Limmatquai 4
8001 Zürich
daycrun.ch

ETH Entrepreneur Club (Rocket Hub)
Building STE,
Stampfenbachstrasse 52/56
8092 Zürich
entrepreneur-club.org/rock-ethub

FabLab Zürich
Zimmerlistraße 6
8004 Zürich
Zürich.fablab.ch

Impact Hub Zürich
Sihlquai 131
8005 Zürich
Zürich.impacthub.ch

Kraftwerk
Seinaustraße 25
8001 Zürich
kraftwerk.host

IFJ Institut für Jungunternehmen startup space
Wiesenstraße 5
8952 Schlieren-Zürich
startup-space.ch

Spaces Bleicherweg
Bleicherweg 10
8002 Zürich
spacesworks.com/Zürich/bleicherweg

Technopark Zürich
Technoparkstraße 1
8005 Zürich
technopark.ch

Experts

Raiffeisen Schweiz
Raiffeisenplatz
9001 St. Gallen
raiffeisen.ch

SAP
startups.sap.com

STARTUP CAMPUS
c/o ZHAW School of
Management and Law
Stadthausstrasse 14
CH-8400 Winterthur
startup-campus.ch

TAMedia
Werdstrasse 21
8004 Zürich
tamedia.ch/startup

Founders

Master21
c/o Impact Hub Zürich
Sihlquai 131
8005 Zürich
master21.academy

On AG
Pfingstweidstraße 106
8005 Zürich
on-running.com

WeAct AG
c/o Impact Hub Zürich
Viaduktstraße 93
8005 Zürich
weact.ch

We Are Play Lab Foundation
Kirchgasse 42
8001 Zürich
wap.rocks

Wingman AG
Lagerstraße 33
8004 Zürich
wingman.ch

Banks

Alternative Bank Switzerland
Kalkbreitestraße 10
Postfach
8036 Zürich
abs.ch

Cler Bank
Uraniastraße 6
8001 Zürich
cler.ch

Clientis
Goethestraße 18
8001 Zürich
zrb.clientis.ch

Credit Suisse
Bahnhofstraße 32
8001 Zürich
credit-suisse.com/ch

Migros Bank
migrosbank.ch

Postfinance
Rennweg 35
8001 Zürich
postfinance.ch

Raiffeisenbank Zürich
Limmatquai 68
8001 Zürich
raiffeisen.ch/zuerich/

UBS
Bahnhofstraße 45
8001 Zürich
ubs.com

Zürcher Kantonalbank
Prime Tower, Hardstraße 201
8005 Zürich
zkb.ch

Zürcher Kantonalbank, ZKB
Bahnhofstraße 9
8001 Zürich
zkb.ch

Coffee Shops and Places with Wifi

169 West
Weststraße 169
8003 Zürich
169west.ch

Auer & Co
Sihlquai 131
8005 Zürich
auer.coffee

Bros Beans & Beats
Gartenhofstraße 24
8004 Zürich
brosbeansbeats.ch

Coffee Shack
Müllerstraße 31
8004 Zürich
coffeeshack.ch

Elle'n'Belle
Limmatstraße 118
8005 Zürich
ellenbelle.ch

Grand Café Lochergut
Badenerstraße 230
8004 Zürich
lochergut.net

Kosmos
Lagerstraße 104
8004 Zürich
kosmos.ch

Kraftwerk Café
Selnaustraße 25
8001 Zürich
kraftwerk.host

sphères
Hardturmstraße 66
8005 Zürich
spheres.cc

directory

Cultural and Traditional Events

Festspiele Zürich
festspiele-zuerich.ch

Internationale Kurzfilmtage Winterthur
kurzfilmtage.ch

Knabenschiessen
knabenschiessen.ch

Kreislauf 345
kreislauf345.ch

Sechseläuten Traditional Spring Festival
sechselaeuten.ch

Silvesterzauber
silvesterzauber.ch

Stadtzürcher Seeüberquerung
seeueberquerung.ch

Street Parade
streetparade.com

Theater Spektakel
theaterspektakel.ch

Weltklasse Zürich – Diamond League
zurich.diamondleague.com

Zürich Film Festival
zff.com

Expat Groups and Meetups

InterNations Zürich
internations.org/zurich-expats

Worldwide People in Zürich
facebook.com/worldwidepeo-pleinzurich/

Zürich Expats
zurichexpats.com

Zürich for you
zurich4you.ch

Flats and Rentals

flatfox
flatfox.ch

Homegate
homegate.ch

Immoscout24
immoscout24.ch

RON ORP Zürich
ronorp.net/zuerich/dach-ue-ber-dem-kopf

WGZIMMER.CH
wgzimmer.ch

Important Government Offices

Commercial Registry Office
Schöntalstraße 5
8022 Zürich
hra.zh.ch

Department of Economic Affairs Office for Economy and Labour
Walchestraße 19
8090 Zürich
location.zh.ch

Migration Office
Berninastraße 45
8090 Zürich
ma.zh.ch

Official Web Portal of Zürich
zuerich.ch

SVA Zürich
Röntgenstraße 17
8087 Zürich
svazurich.ch

Incubators and Accelerators

>>venture>>
venture.ch

ESA BIC Switzerland
c/o ETH Zürich
Stampfenbachstraße 52/56
8092 Zürich
esabic.ch

ETH Innovation and Entrepreneurship Lab (ieLab)
Stampfenbachstraße 52/56
8092 Zürich
ethz.ch/en/industry-and-society/entrepreneurship/ielab

Grow Wädenswil
Einsiedlerstraße 29
8820 Wädenswil
grow-waedenswil.ch

Nexussquared
nexussquared.co

RUNWAY Incubator
Stadthausstraße 14
8400 Winterthur
runway-incubator.ch

SEIF - Driving Social Innovation
Citizen Space
Heinrichstraße 267
8005 Zürich
seif.org

Start Smart Schlieren
Rütistraße 12
8952 Schlieren
start-smart-schlieren.ch

Swiss Life Lab AG
Weinplatz 10
8001 Zürich
sllab.ch

Switzerland Innovation Park Zürich
c/o Stiftung Innovationspark Zürich
Wangenstraße 68
8600 Dübendorf
switzerland-innovation.com/zurich

Venture Kick
venturekick.ch

Z-Kubator
zhdk.ch/zkubator

Insurance Companies

Allianz Suisse
Albisstraße 152
8038 Zürich
allianz.ch

Assura
Algierstraße 1
8048 Zürich
assura.ch

AXA Winterthur
General-Guisan-Straße 40
8400 Winterthur
axa.ch

Comparis
comparis.ch

Concordia (health and accident insurance)
Beatengasse 9
8001 Zürich
concordia.ch

Generali
Mühlebachstraße 7
8008 Zürich
generali.ch

Helsana (health insurance)
Weinbergstraße 5
8000 Zürich
helsana.ch

die Mobiliar
Nüschelerstraße 45
8021 Zürich
mobiliar.ch

Priminfo
priminfo.admin.ch/de/praemien

Sanitas (health insurance)
Jägergasse 3
8004 Zürich
sanitas.com

SVA Zürich (social insurance)
svazurich.ch

Swica (health insurance)
Zollstraße 42
8005 Zürich
swica.ch

Vaudoise
Stampfenbachstraße 40
8006 Zürich
vaudoise.ch

Zürich
Claridenstraße 20
8002 Zürich
zurich.ch

Investors

BlueOrchard
Seefeldstraße 231
8008 Zürich
blueorchard.com

Creathor Ventures
Seehofstraße 6
8008 Zürich
creathor.com

Emerald Technology Ventures
Seefeldstraße 215
8008 Zürich
emerald-ventures.com

GoBeyond
Technoparkstraße 1
8005 Zürich
go-beyond.biz

Redalpine
Pfingstweidstraße 60
8005 Zürich
redalpine.com

responsAbility
Josefstraße 59
8005 Zürich
responsability.com

SICTIC
Stockerstraße 44
8002 Zürich
sictic.ch

**Swiss Private Equity &
Corporate Finance
Association**
seca.ch

Swiss Startup Invest
Dorfstraße 27
8037 Zürich
swiss-startup-invest.ch

Viaduct Ventures
Viaduktstraße 93-95
8005 Zürich
viaduct.ventures

Zühlke Ventures
Wiesenstraße 10a
8952 Schlieren (Zürich)
zuehlke.com

Zukunftsfonds Schweiz
zukunftsfonds.ch

Zürcher Kantonalbank
Prime Tower, Hardstraße 201
8005 Zürich
zkb.ch

Language Schools

Alpha Sprachwelt
Stadelhoferstraße 10
8001 Zürich
alphasprachwelt.ch

Allegra
Löwenstraße 51
8001 Zürich
allegra-schulen.ch
EB Zürich
Riesbachstraße 11
8008 Zürich
eb-zuerich.ch

Benedict-Schule Zürich
Militärstraße 106
8004 Zürich
benedict.ch

**Flying Teachers,
Schweiz, Zürich**
Universitätstraße 86
8006 Zürich
flyingteachers.ch

Italk Sprachschule
Löwenstraße 65-67
8001 Zürich
italksprachschule.com

Migros Klubschule
klubschule.ch

unumondo
c/o Impact Hub
Sihlquai 131
8005 Zürich
unumondo.io

Startup Events

Design Biennale Zürich
designbiennalezurich.ch

Digital Festival
digitalfestival.ch

ETH Entrepreneur Club
entrepreneur-club.org/events

Finance 2.0
finance20.ch

GameZ Festival
gamezfestival.ch

HackZürich
haczurich.com

Impact Hub Zürich
zurich.impacthub.ch/events

**Ludicious Zürich Game
Festival**
ludicious.ch

Maker Faire Zürich
makerfairezurich.ch/en
Meetup
meetup.com/cities/ch/zurich

SICTIC
sictic.ch/events

START Summit
startsummit.ch

Startup Grind Zürich
startupgrind.com/zurich

Startup Weekend Switzerland
startupweekend.ch

startupticker.ch
startupticker.ch/en/events

Swiss ICT Award
swissict-award.ch

Swiss Startup Awards
swiss-startups-awards.ch

TEDxZürich
tedxzurich.com

WORLDWEBFORUM
worldwebforum.com

glossary

A

Accelerator
An organization or program that offers advice and resources to help small businesses grow

Acqui-hire
Buying out a company based on the skills of its staff rather than its service or product

Angel Investment
Outside funding with shared ownership equity

ARR
Accounting (or average) rate of return: calculation generated from net income of the proposed capital investment

B

B2B
(Business-to-Business)
The exchange of services, information and/or products from a business to a business

B2C
(Business-to-Consumer)
The exchange of services, information and/or products
from a business to a consumer

BOM
(Bill of Materials)
The list of the parts or components required to build a product

Bootstrap
To self-fund, without outside investment

Bridge Loan
A short-term loan taken out from between two weeks and three years pending arrangement of longer-term financing

Burn Rate
The amount of money a startup spends

Business Angel
An experienced entrepreneur or professional who provides starting or growth capital for promising startups

C

C-level
Chief position

Canvas Business Model
A template for developing new or documenting existing business models

Cap Table
An analysis of the founders' and investors' percentage of ownership, equity dilution and value of equity in each round of investment

CMO
Chief marketing officer

Cold-Calling
The solicitation of potential customers who were not anticipating such an interaction

Convertible Note/Loan
A type of short-term debt often used by seed investors to delay establishing a valuation for the startup until a later round of funding or milestone

Coworking
A shared working environment

CPA
Cost per action

CPC
Cost per click

Cybersecurity
The body of technologies, processes and practices designed to protect networks, computers, programs and data from attack, damage or unauthorized access

D

Dealflow
Term for investors to refer to the rate at which they receive business proposals

Deeptech
Companies founded on a scientific discovery or meaningful engineering innovation

Diluting
A reduction in the ownership percentage of a share of stock caused by the issuance of new shares

E

Elevator Pitch
A short summary used to quickly define a product or idea

Exit
A way to transition the ownership of a company to another company

F

Fintech
Financial technology

Flex Desk
Shared desk in a space where coworkers are free to move around and sit wherever they like

I

Incubator
Facility established to nurture young startup firms during their early months or years

Installed Base
A reliable indicator of a platform's popularity

IP (Intellectual Property)
Intangible property that is the result of creativity, such as patents, copyrights, etc

**IPO
(Initial Public Offering)**
The first time a company's stock is offered for sale to the public

K

**KPI
(Key Performance Indicator)**
A measurable value that demonstrates how effectively a company is achieving key business objectives

L

Later-Stage
More mature startups/companies

Lean
Refers to 'lean startup methodology;' the method proposed by Eric Ries in his book for developing businesses and startups through product development cycles

M

**M&A
(Mergers and Acquisitions)**
A merger is a combination of two companies to form a new company, while an acquisition is the purchase of one company by another in which no new company is formed

MAU
Monthly active user

MVP
Minimum viable product

P

P2P (Peer-to-Peer)
A network created when two or more PCs are connected and sharing resources without going through a separate server

Pitch Deck
A short version of a business plan presenting key figures

PR-Kit (Press Kit)
Package of pictures, logos and descriptions of your services

Pro-market
A market economy/a capitalistic economy

R

Runtime
The amount of time a startup has survived

S

SaaS
Software as a service

Scaleup
Company that has already validated its product in a market, and is economically sustainable

Seed Funding
First round, small, early-stage investment from family members, friends, banks or an investor

Seed Investor
An investor focusing on the seed round

Seed Round
The first round of funding

Series A/B/C/D
The name of funding rounds coming after the seed stage

Shares
The amount of the company that belongs to someone

Solopreneurs
somebody developing their own personal brand; not a company to hire employees

Startup
Companies under three years old, in the growth stage and becoming profitable (if not already)

SVP
Senior Vice President

T

Term Sheet/Letter of Intent
The document between an investor and a startup including the conditions for financing (commonly non-binding)

U

Unicorn
A company worth over US$1 billion

USP
unique selling point

**UX
(User experience design)**
The process of enhancing user satisfaction by improving the usability, accessibility and pleasure provided in the interaction between the user and the product

V

VC (Venture Capital)
Outside venture capital investment from a pool of investors in a venture capital firm in return for equity

Vesting
Employee rights to employer-provided assets over time, which gives the employee an incentive to perform well and remain with the company

The Entrepreneur's Handbook

STARTUP GUIDE *TRONDHEIM*
STARTUP GUIDE *VIENNA*
STARTUP GUIDE *TEL AVIV*
STARTUP GUIDE *MADRID*
STARTUP GUIDE *COPENHAGEN*
STARTUP GUIDE *PARIS*
STARTUP GUIDE *REYKJAVIK*
STARTUP GUIDE *MUNICH*
STARTUP GUIDE *ZÜRICH*
STARTUP GUIDE *LONDON*
STARTUP GUIDE *LISBON*
STARTUP GUIDE *BERLIN*
STARTUP GUIDE *OSLO*

startupguide.world

Follow us: instagram.com/startupguide.world

About the Guide

Based on traditional guidebooks that can be carried around everywhere,
Startup Guide books help you navigate and connect with different startup
scenes across the globe. Each book is packed with useful information,
exciting entrepreneur stories and insightful interviews with local experts.
As the world of work changes, our mission is to guide, empower and inspire
people to start their own business anywhere. We hope the book will
become your trusted companion as you embark on a new (startup) journey.
Today, Startup Guide books are in 17 different cities in Europe and the
Middle East, including Berlin, London, Tel Aviv, Stockholm, Copenhagen,
Vienna, Lisbon and Paris.

How we make the guides:

To ensure an accurate and trustworthy guide every time, we team up with a city partner that is
established in the local startup scene. Then we ask the local community to nominate startups,
co-working spaces, founders, incubators and established businesses to be featured through
an online submission form. Based on the results, these submissions are narrowed down to the
top fifty companies and individuals. Afterwards, the local advisory board – which is selected
by our community partner and consists of key players in the local startup community – votes
for the final selection so there's a balanced representation of industries and startup stories in
each book. The local community partner then works in close collaboration with our editorial
and design team in Berlin to help research, organize interviews with journalists as well as plan
photoshoots with photographers. Finally, all content is reviewed, edited and put into the book's
layout by the Startup Guide team in Berlin and Lisbon before going for print in Berlin.

Where to find us:

The easiest way to get your hands on a Startup Guide book is to order it from our online shop:
startupguide.world/shop

If you prefer to do things in real life, drop by one of the fine retailers listed on the stockists page
on our website.
Want to become a stockist or suggest a store? Get in touch here: **sales@startupguide.world**

#startupeverywhere

Startup Guide is a creative content and publishing company founded by Sissel Hansen in 2014. We produce guidebooks and tools to help entrepreneurs navigate and connect with different startup scenes across the globe. As the world of work changes, our mission is to guide, empower and inspire people to start their own business anywhere. Today, Startup Guide books are in 17 different cities in Europe and the Middle East, including Berlin, London, Tel Aviv, Stockholm, Copenhagen, Vienna, Lisbon and Paris. We also have two physical stores in Berlin and Lisbon to promote and sell products by startup. Startup Guide is a 20-person team based in Berlin and Lisbon. Visit our site for more: **startupguide.world/**

Want to get more info, be a partner or say hello?

Shoot us an email here **info@startupguide.world**

Join us and **#startupeverywhere**

The Startup Guide Stores

Whether it's sniffing freshly printed books or holding an innovative product, we're huge fans of physical experiences. That's why we opened two stores—one in Lisbon another in Berlin. Not only do the stores showcase our books and curated products, they're also our offices and a place for the community to come together to share wows and hows. Say hello!

Berlin:
Waldemarstraße 38, 10999 Berlin
Mon-Fri: 10h-18h
+49 (0)30-37468679
berlin@startupguide.world

Lisbon:
R. Rodrigues de Faria
103, 1300 - 501 Lisboa
Mon-Fri: 10h-18h
+351 21 354 5154
lisbon@startupguide.world

With thanks to our **content sponsors**

Zürcher Hochschule
für Angewandte Wissenschaften

With thanks to our **Community Partner**

Event Partner
/ WORLDWEBFORUM

The WORLDWEBFORUM is a leading business conference for digital transformation and thought leadership in Europe. Every year, visionaries, entrepreneurs and investors from Silicon Valley share their insights and experiences in Zürich.

More than 2,000 C-level attendees from all over the world are inspired by the WORLDWEBFORUM every year. Since its inception, CEO and founder Fabian Hediger and his team have managed to attract top speakers, entrepreneurs and academics year after year. Among them were big names, including Apple cofounder Steve Wozniak; the inventor of the internet Sir Tim Berners-Lee; former Apple and Pepsi CEO John Scully; and Pixar cofounder, president of Disney Animation Studios and four-time Oscar-winner Ed Catmull.

The first day of the 2018 conference was dedicated to keynote speakers, while industry-specific challenges in verticals were discussed on the second day. These included topics such as finance/blockchain, food chain, retail, augmented reality, IoT, real estate (Digit!mmo), the future of work, responsive cities, tourism, the cloud and more.

"More than eighty percent of the GNP in continental Europe is generated in the old economy. This is a time bomb!" says Fabian Hediger. Google, Facebook, Apple, Microsoft and Amazon are the most powerful companies worldwide, and they are driving economic globalization and are admired for this. However, Europe is fighting politically against these internet pioneers because they are challenging the status quo and disrupting both regulations and ultimately the nation state. There is much to learn from these disruptive companies.

Blockchain technology, for example, is an alternative financial system without monetary policy, and government regulation is currently on the rise. Private companies and investors have never been able to allocate their resources or gain influence across borders so easily, making the nation state and its institutions redundant. These were the fundamental topics for the last WORLDWEBFORUM 2018.

Be inspired by digital leaders, learn from disruptive business models and expand your horizon. Don't miss the opportunity to take part in one of the most important conferences in Europe next year. Visit worldwebforum.com for more information.

WHERE NEXT?